How To Books General Editor Roland Seymour

SURVIVE
AT COLLEGE

David Acres

Northcote House

Acknowledgements
Many students have contributed ideas to this book. Ex-students Mark and Michelle Brockbank helped me organise ideas, researched information and alerted me to ideas. I'm grateful to them both as I am to my counsellor colleagues at Plymouth Polytechnic. Susan Gilderdale has contributed much of the material for Chapter 4 'Feeding Yourself' and Peter Aizlewood, John Jenkinson and Peter Jones have offered comments and encouragement. Finally I'd like to thank Mark Hannon for his sharp cartoons.

© *Copyright 1987 by David Acres*

First published in 1987 by Northcote House Publishers Ltd., Harper & Row House, Estover Road, Plymouth PL6 7PZ, United Kingdom. Tel: Plymouth (0752) 705251. Telex: 45635.

British Library Cataloguing in Publication Data
Acres, David
    How to survive at college — (How to books).
    1. College students — Great Britain —
    Life skills guides
I. Title
378'.198   LA637.7

ISBN 0-7463-0507-9

Printed and bound in Great Britain

Contents

1
Ready to go?

Although the majority of students survive their time at University, Polytechnic and other colleges of Higher Education, many have tough times along the way. Others don't survive, choosing to drop out as 5 to 10% do each year. Another 5 to 10% fail their course exams (higher percentages on some technology and science courses) and have to leave. Others don't enjoy the experience of college, facing problems they find difficult to overcome.

This book is devoted to how to survive at college and *live life to the full whilst you're there*. It becomes easier to do both if you ensure you're ready to go, by asking yourself three questions

● Are you going to the right college?
● Have you prepared yourself for what it will be like?
● Have you got what you need to take with you?

You can use the three Checklists that follow to check that you really are ready to go and to allay any last minute doubts you may have.

Is it the right college?
Check your answers to these four questions to see how clear you are in your decision.

● **How much do you know about the college?**
  Have you gained a clear picture of its layout, size, facilities, students union building, library, accommodation provision, welfare and counselling provision? Do you know enough about its distance from your home and transport time as a result of your visiting it? Have you seen where you'll be taught and met some staff?

● **How much do you know about the course?**
  Do you know its structure, year-by-year? Do you know the timetable, weekly attendance requirement, options structure and assessments.

Have you met the staff, some students and seen where you'll be taught?

- **Do you understand the demands of the subject?**
  Are you clear about the nature of the subject and how it differs, if at all, from A level/BTEC subjects? Do you understand what each term means? eg that Quantitative Methods means Mathematics above O level/GCSE standards.

- **Do you really want to go?**
  Are you clear about what you want and expect from college? Have you made your *own* decision to go? Are you ready to be a student for another 2, 3 or 4 years?

- **Do you have doubts?**
  If you have doubts as a result of thinking about these, or other questions, then you can re-check your decisions by using the companion volume of this book *'How to Get to College', David Acres, Pitman.*

Check your preparedness
You can use this Checklist to review how well prepared for college you feel and how many practical steps you've taken before you go.

- **Have you made the most of available careers help?**
  eg careers interviews, school or college guidance programme, LEA careers officers?

- **Have you talked to the right people?**
  eg someone who's studied the subject or is on the course, ex-students/pupils, those who know the college or town, other students in the same position as yourself (mature, overseas)?

- **Visited the college and geographical environs?**
  eg attended open days, visits or advisory interviews, looked around the town, stayed with friends or relatives nearby to acclimatise yourself?

- **Do you feel psychologically prepared?**
  eg do you feel ready to go, positive and informed? Are you reading *'How to Survive at College'* to enable you to anticipate hassle, shared hopes and fears?

● **Have you sought out useful contacts?**
eg it can help to have the name of someone from your home town or school, a Great Aunt Emma or a friend of the family in the local area. Phone numbers and ease of contact can help if you feel low, to enable a short visit or overnight stay.

● **Have you prepared for the course?**
eg read some of the recommended books (or at least some pages from them), given some thought to the content of the syllabus and course structure?

● **Have you seriously considered an alternative?**
eg a year off or employment are well worth considering rather than unthinkingly staying on the conveyor belt into higher education.

● **How are your skills at managing yourself?**
eg sorting out your money and handling it, organising your own time during the 168 hour week, or using effective study skills?

● **If it's a late decision to go, or a late choice of course, are you sure about it?**
eg have you got a clear picture of what you are letting yourself in for? How informed do you feel about the course, the college, the town, etc?

CHECKLIST: WHAT TO TAKE WITH YOU

- **Maps and instructions**
  Maps of the campus, town, surrounding countryside, routes from your home; instructions for finding your accommodation and college.

- **Course information**
  All essential information about where to go, what to do and when, who's who, induction programmes and reading lists.

- **Cash**
  Money to see you through 3-4 weeks, assuming delays in cash arriving from LEA or parents.

- **Specialised equipment**
  Any particular equipment, clothing or textbook you've been told to acquire before the course commences.

- **An alarm clock**
  Particularly useful if you have lectures at 9 am.

- **Stationery**
  Students sometimes find that the odd pen, piece of paper, file is helpful.

- **Personal possessions**
  Taking some of your home comforts can help make a place feel like yours. Posters, a favourite book, your stereo, a hot water-bottle, a coffee cup, your teddy (!) are examples.

Off you go
Thus prepared and equipped, you can bid *au revoir* to loved ones and prepare to enter the first term.

2
Surviving the first term

The first term at college is likely to be one of the most memorable periods of your life. Students use various words to describe their first four or six weeks in college: 'colourful', 'exciting', 'confusing', 'disillusioning', 'frightening', 'stressful'. Whatever word you'll be using to describe your experience, one thing is certain — the first term at college is an important period of your life.

Why confusion?

The 'confusion' is, in part, a reflection of the complexity of what is going on. There are so many pieces of information to digest — not just about your subjects either. There is informaton about how the college works, who the people are, where places can be found.

You will have the adjustments of organising yourself and being entirely responsible for planning and using time. There are dozens, if not hundreds, of new people you'll meet. There may also be confusion, too, over what you and others are doing there: about the value of it all and where it is leading. Some of the colleges may not help in this way, for they may not know where they're going either and have no clear idea of what type of educational environment they are trying to create.

Guidelines through the confusion

This chapter will take you through some of the key information of the first term introducing some key events and key people as well as some of the issues that may occur.

Although the vast majority of students make it through the term, not without the ups and downs described (and see also our 'Snakes and Ladders' illustration on p.12), some decide to leave voluntarily, to discontinue. Chapter 13 also contains guidelines and key information for those who may at some point wonder if they really want to carry on.

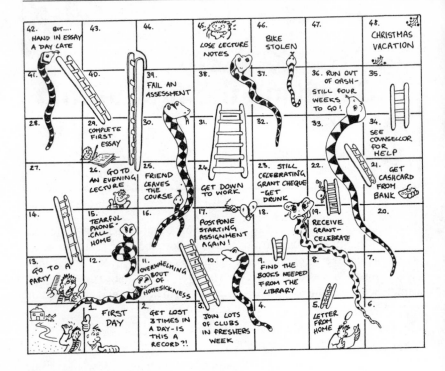

FIRST THINGS FIRST

First impressions

For those of you who have visited the college or town before the start of term, there will have already been opportunity to form a — hopefully — clear impression of the place. You will recognise some buildings or sights and, in consequence, the place will not be entirely strange to you. If you are arriving in the area for the first time, it may well feel strange, even hostile, in its unfamiliarity.

As much as anything, the weather can exaggerate these first impressions. Arriving in daylight on a warm early autumn day can show off the college and town at its best. At night and in the pouring rain you are less likely to be impressed.

The first look at your room is another important first impression. Don't expect it to appear homely without your possessions, posters and nicknacks. It's more likely to appear stark, with the remains of another student's Blutack on the walls.

First meetings with people

Your first meetings with people can make a lot of difference to how you feel — the attitudes of the passer-by you ask for directions, of the warden, porter, landlady or landlord who greets you, will all have an effect. Even the course tutor can set the tone of your course by the way the first meeting is conducted. Being on the receiving end of a warm smile and a friendly word helps the feeling of belonging to develop.

Your room mate or fellow residents are among the first people you'll be meeting and they are likely to be important people in everyday life. So, too, are others you meet in college in your first few days, particularly those on your course.

Finding your way around

So many college sites are confusing when you first arrive. Sometimes it's because they are inadequately signposted. At other times the modern buildings and walkways can appear to be identical to each other, until you learn your way through the maze. Some colleges acknowledge this by attempts to colour code routes through a building or site. Different coloured stair-rails will indicate the different exits from a building. Colour lines on paving stones will show you the route to particular buildings.

Three tips will cut down early difficulties. Tear out the map in the prospectus and carry it around with you. Then locate the key buildings — library, the teaching block, the Students Union and, if applicable, your hall of residence. Note the buildings nearby and the paths you tread between them. Finally, ask others the way. It's a good way to get to talk to people.

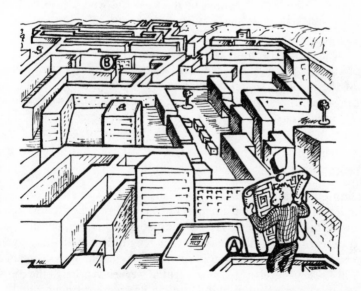

Talk to people

The sheer numbers of other people can feel quite overwhelming in the first days of college, but that is one feeling you are all likely to have in common. You are also all likely to have a hesitance or shyness about talking to those in the group with whom you haven't yet spoken. You may also be wondering what to say. There are usually two fundamental things that every student wants to share with others. The first is the individual experience of settling in, accommodation or how it was found and first impressions of people and places. The second is getting to know other people sufficiently well to form and share friendships.

In those first days and weeks of the course take the chance to talk to as many people as possible. Many conversations will be superficial; many relationships passing ones, but from them real friendships will emerge.

JOIN THE QUEUE

One of the consequences of the demand for higher education is the large size of the first-year intake in many colleges. As a result, in the first few days in particular, you may seem to be spending half your life in queues.

You may queue for *enrolment,* which is when you officially register as a student of the college. You may queue to enrol with a doctor at a *medical centre. Collecting your grant* will most likely involve another queue. Grants are frequently delayed by two or three weeks (or more in some cases), so returning to a particular room or the Registry (who distribute them) to see if it has arrived is a very common event.

Queues may also form for *NUS Student registration cards.* This entitles you to cheap travel, discounts on theatre concerts and even records, books etc in certain stores. You may well also need it for security checks at the door of the Students Union building.

But the other times you will really notice the crowds are when you are waiting to get in or out of lecture theatres and classrooms. It can feel like travelling on the London underground in the rush hour.

MEETING THE STAFF

Induction courses

An induction course is an attempt by the course team to introduce themselves, the subjects, the assessment methods, the support staff and other aspects of college life. They range in length from half a day to one or two weeks, indeed, even longer in courses with complex course organisation. Some colleges even organise residential weekends prior to the course and these are an excellent way of getting to know other students and the course staff on an informal basis.

At worst, these induction courses can involve you sitting passively for hours with a group of strangers, listening to another collection of individual strangers talk a great deal. Many people will say, 'Come and see us if you have a problem', but you may be confused about who you are supposed to see if you are in difficulties (see Chapter 13 for guidelines).

The best induction courses give you the opportunity to talk regularly to other students on your course. They give you a chance to meet staff informally. Trips around town may be included and certainly some social event.

Certainly, during induction courses, you'll begin to get the feel of the college organisation and the staff you'll meet.

The staff — and their college roles
In many colleges there are as many back-up staff as there are academic staff. During your average week you will be meeting kitchen and bar staff, janitors (porters and security staff), library assistants, cleaners and members of the administrative staff. Their attitudes — and yours towards them — become an important part of the atmosphere of being at college.

However, the atmosphere created by the attitude of academic staff, those who manage the college and those in student support services are likely to be more important in your overall experience at college. Many courses (but not all) are having to cope with larger numbers of students than in the past, and this can affect staff attitudes as well as their morale.

Staff morale — a cautionary note
Cutbacks on finance, closure or threat of closure of colleges, amalgamations and reorganisation of certain colleges, and the fear of job losses have profoundly affected the morale of college staff in recent years. The stress experienced by many staff is real, particularly if they are coping with larger student numbers involving extra work in course planning, in marking assignments and in examinations.

Extra students will also place a strain on facilities. There may not be enough equipment or books to go round. Sweaty lecture rooms with students sitting on the floor and the busy corridors outside will not enhance the college atmosphere.

Staff frustration
The majority of college staff are well qualified, conscientious people who want to do the best job possible. They feel frustrated when they are unable to do so. It may increase their pre-occupation with staff concerns like where course funds will be coming from or when they can take early retirement.

It will mean that not all the staff you meet will be wonderful, warm human beings interested in their individual students. Fortunately, however, there are enough people around who care, who show they care and will make what time they can to help you. The following guide may help you spot the most useful people in your college.

A guide to college staff

The following light-hearted characterisations of lecturing staff are not mutually exclusive, ie an individual lecturer may have more than one of the characteristics.

The academic subject enthusiast

The lovable eccentric in a world of his own. He's either capable of filling you with a love of the subject — or unable to teach anybody anything.

The researcher

Chances are he's pushing back the frontiers of knowledge. Probably knows more about the lesser-spotted fangle-worzeled sputtock than any man in the Western World. With luck, he'll be passing on useful, relevant and up-to-date knowledge and ideas. Without luck, he'll find that lecturing and students get in the way of the 'real work'.

The students-matter type

When he's good he's very good but when he's bad . . . At best, an enormous source of support and encouragement, capable of changing, for the better, your attitude towards yourself, your work and others. Even below par he may be useful to have around.

The international jet-setter

You will probably see more of this lecturer on television than at his lectures. His next book is due out soon. You may find people asking, 'Didn't old so-and-so used to work here?'

The teacher type

More concerned about education in a wider context than teaching his subject. He is enthusiastic about clear communication and improving learning ability. Nevertheless, he may forget entirely what his subject specialism is.

The take-it-or-leave-it type

Knows the subject very well. Heavily into Darwin. If you're up to it, you'll immediately understand his explanation and example of a point. He is concerned that the quality of students is not what it used to be. These days a lot of them just can't keep up. Still it's not his fault, is it?

The course co-ordinator/course tutor
The great solver of practical day-to-day problems — if you can catch him. Often seen running like the wind, files under his arm, for today's Course/Planning/Resubmission Committee. A hard man to pin down.

The socialiser
Here is a lecturer who acknowledges the value of meeting students socially for a meal, wine and cheese evening, game of pool or a drink. On the other hand, he could be just trying to chat up the freshers.

The personal tutor
If you're lucky, a solid support, academically and in many other ways. Even so, you may well be in too large a group to see him very often, or even get to know him well at all. Alternatively, he may be someone who didn't want to be one and doesn't know (or want to know) what to say when he meets you and so doesn't do so very often.

The easing-down-to-retirement type or 'thank-God-it's-only-another-12-months' type
You can guess the behaviour of this one.

The politician
At best he will forge a good deal for colleagues and students by working hard at college politics. But just as likely he may be an in-fighter who loses sight of the real issue and is more pre-occupied with so-and-so's next move.

The education-is-a-business type
Thrusting, ambitious, manager-type, interested in efficiency, maximising staff-student ratios and statistics. Attracts funds, efficiency and reputation if he's good. A bad one will be disinterested in individual students and expects some 'wastage'. Probably looks like a banker or an accountant.

. . . and finally

The Vice-Chancellor/Director/Principal/Dean
May be seen once a year, if you keep a sharp look out. Particularly concerned about the 'image' of the college and money and resource issues, to which end much time is spent in meetings. They may be rather frightened of students, particularly if they don't meet them that often.

THE STUDENTS UNION

Discovering the Students Union

Students Union (SUs) vary in size and location. Some campus colleges have common rooms or bars or games rooms scattered around the campus in residential blocks as well as a centralised Union building. More typically, one building acts as the main social centre for students.

SUs use their funds to provide bars, TV areas, lounges, refectories and canteens, shops, games rooms, washing facilities for clothes, showers and toilets and many other facilities. They also use funds to pay the full and part-time staff who manage and run the SUs buildings and facilities. Other money is used to subsidise a wide range of student clubs and societies. In addition every SU has its own — usually weekly — newspaper/ magazine.

Using the SU

During the first term there will be many good reasons to use the SU. They exist for you to meet friends, eat, have a drink, pick up your weekly SU newspaper, buy stationery, look at noticeboards to find what's on, check pigeonholes for messages and letters, and for many other purposes.

Further, in the first few weeks of term there will be many events for all students, but particularly to welcome and involve *you* as a new student.

FRESHERS WEEK

'Freshers Week' (it may go under other names such as 'Intro Week') will normally take place within a few days of your arrival, often in the first week of October. During this week there will be special events — *The Freshers Ball* is typical. Upmarket colleges may make this into quite a formal and extravagant occasion. Most colleges have a less formal occasion(!) but all the same make it into a special event.

During the week there will be other entertainment. This will include visiting rock bands, discos run by the SU or various clubs and societies, or wine and cheese evenings. The bars are likely to be granted an extension for the big occasions and it is common for the brewery who finances the bar to offer some promotion on drink during that week.

As well as all this entertainment there is often some more formal welcome for you. Typically, new students are invited to a gathering addressed by the College Vice Chancellor, Director, Principal, Dean, etc. This may not be the most entertaining, or informative, meeting of the week.

In this week you'll form your first impressions of the SU building. It may not always be favourable. It is often stark and bearing the marks of heavy use by thousands of students. It will also be very crowded, thousands of people may be moving in and out between the hours of 12 and 2 each day, for example. Opinions about the SU are often strongly felt, and may develop early.

Joining clubs and societies
During Freshers Week there is also a special afternoon and/or evening at which the various clubs and societies of the Union set up stalls to invite you to join their ranks. This can be the most important event of the week and, for some, the term.

This is a chance for you to set up a social life for yourself outside of your course. For a small cost you can join as many clubs and societies as you want. The choice is likely to be very wide — political groups or sports and outdoor activity groups or societies based around hobbies and interests.

The chances are you'll join more clubs than you'll ever be able to attend so try to be selective.

WEEKENDS

Weekends at college
The first few weekends at college are often more difficult because they lack the structure of the weekday college routine. If Friday and Saturday night social life and Saturday shopping occupy some of the weekend, other parts of it can feel empty.

Many students, even the most conscientious, give themselves a day off completely at the weekend — Saturday is the usual choice. They will also plan to study for some of the time, but sometimes a full social weekend (or an empty one) can get in the way of studying.

Sunday
Sunday is a challenge. It is often the biggest problem day. For many students, some of it is used for study, particularly when Monday deadlines are involved. What Sundays demand is the maximum amount of self-organisation for the hours and hours of time without a structure unless you give them one. Lying in bed is a common structure students use.

If you find you've experienced a lonely, homesick sort of weekend, talk about and prepare the following weekend before it arrives. Simple ideas like arranging to meet someone to go for a walk or do some studying or to eat or go to a film or for a drink can brighten the day considerably and act as a reward for completed work.

Weekends away
If you are studying away from home the issue of when and how often

to go home at weekends crops up in the first term. It's a matter of trial and error and a question of whether you can afford to go.

One suggestion that works for many students is to go home after about four weeks. The benefits lie in putting home into perspective. During the first weeks, home can often be viewed with rose-coloured spectacles; a weekend at home can help you see and feel it as it really is.

Others hanker after a visit home week-by-week, counting off the days to the weekend. Many students go home frequently at weekends, even weekly. The problem lies in the unsettling effects of these frequent visits. Mondays become more difficult as the return to college requires adjustment. You miss out on the weekend world of other students, making it more difficult to re-enter groups and maintain relationships. Try to monitor carefully whether your gains in returning home are outweighing the losses.

IF ALL IS NOT GOING WELL . . .

Phone calls home can be very helpful to both your parents and yourself. But often they can also be distressing for you both, as you realise how upset, miserable, lonely or uncertain you feel about some aspects of college. You can both be very aware of the distance between you. So talk to someone on the spot as well.

Any friends you've made can help. You may well find you have some feelings and concerns in common, but friends might not be enough of a help. They may be rather close to your situation themselves, not be that objective and have a limited knowledge or experience of the problem to draw upon. So approach one of the college staff who may offer help, even if you don't know what the matter is or are not sure if you'd know what to say or feel you'll burst into tears. Chapter 13 tells you more about what to do if you feel you must leave.

Accommodation

Your accommodation can have a considerable influence — negative or positive — on your feelings during these early days. So the next chapter considers the advantages and disadvantages of the main forms of student accommodation, ie living at home, halls of residence, lodgings and self-catering. It examines how to find flats, bedsits and houses, the main forms of self-catering accommodation. It includes comparisons of costs and guidance on housing benefit. As well as guidance about domestic chores and any legal disputes you may have, you'll find a checklist for rating your accommodation.

3
The best accommodation deals

Living at Home

Advantages of living at home

- It's often much cheaper than any other form of accommodation. If you are living in the family home any contribution you make to the family budget is likely to be far less than if you are living away from home.

- It enables continuity in family life. You can live in familiar places and meet those friends who remain at home.

- You've still got the opportunity to meet new people and experience new worlds as a student in higher education, whilst retaining the security of familiar people.

- You retain your option to move out from home at some stage of your course, although you'll gain no additional LEA cash help to do so.

- As a mature student, it reduces the costs and hassles involved in having, and maintaining, two homes, particularly if separated from your spouse and/or children.

Disadvantages of living at home

- With your friends away you may have the feeling of losing out on an experience.

- You may feel restricted in fully joining in the total social, academic and cultural world of other students who live away from home.

- Some loss of independence and freedom of life-style may be involved. This may influence comings-and-goings, whom you feel able to meet and where.

- Considerable time (and cost) may be tied up in long journeys across cities like London or counties like Devon, if your home is not located close to the college you are attending.

Halls of residence

Advantages of halls of residence

- A best buy in value. You'll normally get your own single room, with adequate study facilities (although storage of books, papers and possessions may be a problem). Included in the cost will be your heating, use of a shared kitchen, bathroom, shower and toilet facilities and any laundry or other shared areas provided.

- At best, a great deal of independence. You can come and go as you please with your own access keys.

- There are real opportunities for forming friendships and a good social life. Floors and landings with six to twelve people sharing the facilities can develop a self-help atmosphere of their own, sharing cooking, worries, tasks and social life.

Disadvantages of halls of residence

- It can feel claustrophobic with so many people of the same age living together. You can find yourself loving your neighbour less as the result of the way community facilities are used and abused — kitchens are a frequent conflict point. Noise can be a problem. Late night parties elsewhere in the block or revellers returning from a good night out can lead to tiredness and frustration, particularly as there is a tendency to stay up late sharing coffees, etc, and conversation.

- Conversely, isolation can also be a problem, particularly where no common room exists. The need for company, for someone to talk to, is reflected by doors being propped open so that passers-by can more easily be seen, spoken to and invited in.

- Some colleges in city centres have acquired unwanted *blocks of flats* from city councils or other bodies. These have been taken over for student use, which is more appropriate. Whilst they have some of the same advantages of other halls of residence, their location can sometimes be in an area where students aren't necessarily well accepted.

Lodgings

Advantages of lodgings

- It can provide a home-from-home to ease the transition in going to college in that meals will be cooked for you at set times and a clear structure will be there in everyday life to act as a secure base for your studying.

- You can save time in that someone else is shopping for food and cooking for you.

- Lodgings also bring you into direct contact with other age groups and a cross-section of humanity, unlike halls where the problems you face are likely to be shared by the same age group and can lead to an exaggeration of their importance.

- Successfully making, and maintaining, relationships with your landlady/landlord requires mutual respect, understanding and tolerance. If you achieve it, it helps prepare you for living with your peers in self-catering accommodation later.

- Living in lodgings for up to a year or so before moving into self-catering can be a useful half-way house on the road to fuller independence.

Disadvantages of lodgings

- The prime disadvantage of lodgings lies in the restrictions on living your life exactly as you wish to live it. You are not likely to be the most popular lodger if you don't turn up for meals or return unsteadily, singing 'You'll never walk alone' at 3 am having forgotten your key.

- You will be living in someone else's home, which may well have a different feel to living in your own. Privacy can be a problem too, at times, as can living with the noise level of having a young family or a loud TV.

- Lodgings can be quite a distance from college. In London this could mean an hour or more's travel each way, or in other towns, 6 miles or so. This can be a major disadvantage. (Try to choose the best lodgings that are most accessible to college.)

Self-Catering

The advantages of self-catering

- In good self-catering accommodation you will have an independent lifestyle with the minimum number of restrictions.

- Friends can visit and stay overnight. You can choose to eat what you like and when you like, within the mutually agreed times for using any shared kitchen facilities.

- At best you'll be living with friends and able to both enjoy life together and support each other through more difficult times. It's more difficult to be lonely in flats and houses.

The disadvantages of self-catering

- With some honourable exceptions, students are one of the groups who live in the worst of society's housing. Tales of dampness, poor decoration, minimal facilities, overcrowding and poor furnishings are commonplace in bedsits, flats and houses. There are also some excessive rents paid for some of these poor facilities.

- Even the relative freedom in self-catering accommodation can be a mixed blessing as it demands a degree of self-organisation that can be difficult and time-consuming.

- Conflicts and day-to-day disputes are not unknown either, both within the bedsit, flat or house and with the landlord or lady.

- When living alone in a bedsit, you can feel isolated and lonely.

Other accommodation

When searching for a place to live you may find you can *sleep at a friend's accommodation* for short periods of time. Sleeping on floors or sofas in other people's living areas can only be a temporary arrangement, as can *sleeping in cars,* or *sleeper caravanettes,* which some students use at the beginning of courses. Others use *homes of relatives* to stay in for some of their college stay, particularly when they first arrive. It is quite common to stay in *bed and breakfast* accommodation for a few days whilst searching for more permanent accommodation. A very few affluent students can afford stays in *hotels* for periods of time during their stay at college. Other short-term accommodation may be available at sought-after *short-stay hostels* in cities like London. Check your college or SU welfare officer for information about their availability.

Some students live in a *caravan* on a residential site, if they can find one with adequate facilities within accessible distance from college. The international organisations *YMCA* and *YWCA* have residential hall-of-residence type accommodation centrally sited in many cities. They are popular with both males and females and are often not single-sex in intake. Self-service restaurants are usually attached, providing reasonably-priced food.

Finding self-catering accommodation
There is an enormous amount of movement and change in self-catering accommodation. If you stay in one house, flat or bedsit for a year you're likely to see a lot of people come and go. Although you'll need your share of luck to find good quality accommodation, you'll also need to be persistent and follow one or more of these tips.

Tips

- *Act quickly* when you hear of accommodation which sounds as though it's what you want (it may not be). Speed is of the essence. Flats often go to the first reputable team to get to the landlord/lady.

- Catch the earliest edition of the local *evening* or *daily paper* in which the majority of accommodation offered is advertised. If necessary, go to where the paper is printed and collect one of the first copies off the presses. Ring immediately. It still won't guarantee you are first in the queue, but it's a familiar exercise for many students and can pay off.

- *Search in groups.* Split up tasks between you to share the work of looking.

- *Take note of word-of-mouth tips.* They are the major source of information about bedsits, flats and houses in many colleges. Many places are found this way.

- *Use your college accommodation office.* They tend to be much criticised for having nothing suitable available, but it's often a matter of being in the office at the time when some new flat or house has been offered. Regularly calling in can help maximise your chance of getting such a place and you won't have to pay an agency fee.

- Do the rounds of the *accommodation agencies,* checking to see if new accommodation is available.

- *Get to know your landlord or lady.* They may own several properties or be in contact with other landlords.

- *Check cards displayed* in shop windows and in your students union or accommodation office. Be prepared to join an existing group who are seeking a third, fourth or fifth resident to share the rent. Joining an existing group is a risk but can be very successful.

- *Use your contacts with the local community* via a local choir, sports group or church to pick up tips on what's available or who to contact.

- Be prepared (if you can afford it) to *pay a retainer* from the end of one term to the beginning of the.next to secure a property you're keen on.

Accommodation costs vary

Apart from the annual escalation of the cost of living, accommodation costs vary according to a number of factors:

- geographical area
- type of accommodation
- demand for particular types of accommodation
- facilities included in the payment you make
- numbers of people sharing the accommodation

There are wide variations in the costs of accommodation even within a particular town. Thus, for example, your share in a house could cost anything between £11 and £35 per week, even where the average cost may be £22. That said, the table below will give you some cost guidelines.

HOUSING COSTS COMPARED 1982-1988		
WEEKLY COSTS OUTSIDE LONDON FOR:	1982/3	1987/8
Halls of Residence (Single Room)	£16	£21
Self Catering (bedsits, flats, houses)		
— Single Room	£15	£22
— Shared Room	£14	£19
Full Board Lodgings (Bed, breakfast and evening meal, plus weekend main meals)		
— Single Room	£27	£34
— Shared Room	£25	£31

Notes

- London rates are considerably higher for all but halls of residence. Add £8 or £10 per week at least.

- Bedsits can be more expensive than other types of self-catering eg £30 to £40 per week.

- Halls of residence vary in facilities and costs. Some CHEs and Universities still include meals in your payment (even if you don't eat them). Others charge you separately for heating. A particular college may have different rates for separate halls, according to their facilities. There are a few halls with shared rooms, for which rents are reduced. Examples of the variation of costs in 1987 were:

Bristol Polytechnic	£25 pw
Kent University	£23 pw
Goldsmiths College	£27 pw
Middlesex Poly	£25 pw

and at the lower end

Leeds University	£13 pw
Nottingham University	£12.50 pw
Central London Poly	£20 pw
University College	£19 pw

Saving money

You can save money by careful choice of your accommodation and its heating system. Here are some key tips.

- Search around, comparing costs, before you commit yourself to a place. Costs vary enormously eg a share in a house.

- If you are living in rented self-catering accommodation outside of halls of residence, make sure you claim any housing benefit entitlement. *See* p.28.

- Check for hidden costs in any signed agreement between tenant and landlord eg excessive deductions from your deposit (which may well be £100 +) for minor damage to paintwork.

- Have a communal fund, to which all tenants contribute on a pay-as-you-go basis, week-by-week to cover the costs of telephone calls, heating, etc. Three-monthly bills can often be difficult to pay otherwise, especially when someone has a girl/boyfriend in another country and keeps using the phone for contact!

Cutting heating and electricity costs

Electric bar fires are common in self-catering accommodation and tend to be expensive, particularly when paid for on a coin meter. For example, keeping a single bar on for a day can cost you two pounds or more during cold spells.

Try to save money in cold weather by:

- Wearing extra clothing. Several layers of thinner clothing are more effective than one thick sweater. Look seriously at buying thermal underwear.

- Keep doors closed and ensure doors and windows are draught-proofed. It costs little to cut down an icy blast from outside. Drawing curtains on winter evenings also keeps heat in.

- Investigate cheaper forms of heating than your existing system. Most forms of heating have some drawbacks eg smell, dirt, risk of fire but it may be worth checking on paraffin stoves or Calor gas heaters for example.

- Turn off your lights and electric appliances when you're not using them.

- Check the actual costs of any metered use of electricity or gas. Raise any apparent high costs with your landlord/lady and work out a refund system. The Electricity or Gas Board could also check the setting.

Housing Benefit

Housing benefit is payable where the cost of your rent, in the private housing market, entitles you to receive cash help from the government. The benefit is fixed to operate once your rent has reached a certain threshold, annually adjusted. You can't claim it for anything but rent (not rates, electricity, water charges or anything else you pay to your landlord/lady). Neither can you claim if you are in accommodation run by your college eg a hall of residence or college house (unless you're there in the summer vacation, for which period you may claim).

Two Kinds of Housing Benefit

- Claims not linked to Supplementary Benefit, payable as *Standard Housing Benefit*.
- Claims by those receiving Supplementary Benefit, for which the DHSS issues a certificate authorising a local authority to pay the claimant's rent and rates. It is called *Certificated Housing Benefit*.

You may be entitled to both forms of benefit at different points in the year eg standard benefit in term time and certificated in the summer vacation. You cannot claim *standard* benefit for Christmas and Easter vacations or for *retainer* payments made to a landlord/lady for the vacation periods.

How to claim and seek advice

- Call in at your Welfare Office, located in the SU, Student Services, or both. They'll be able to give you guidance on whether you can claim, where to go and what to do.

- Your local Housing Advice Centre, usually located in the town hall or civic centre will also offer guidance, as will the local Citizens' Advice Bureau.

- To claim standard housing benefit contact your local Council Treasury and pick up a rent allowance form (Form RR 1). Sometimes a separate form is used, especially designed for students. Claims for certificated housing benefit must go to the DHSS.

  Some students receive the cash help on a weekly basis, others at the end of term in a lump sum. Enquire into how it is paid once your claim has been accepted.

- The *NUS Welfare Manual (Annual)* will be kept by your local Welfare Office and provides detailed and clear guidelines.

Disputes and legal tangles

Disputes over rent, damage to property, notice to quit, who is entitled to be living in the home and the repairs or redecoration required are among the common causes of conflict between landlady/landlord and tenant.

To cut down the chances of this happening to you:

● Ensure you have a clear legal tenancy agreement when you agree to become the tenant. SUs, local housing advice centres and other agencies will give you guidelines as to what you should or should not agree. They might also be useful if a dispute arises that cannot be talked through.

● When a difficulty arises, try to talk to the landlord/lady as soon as possible. Explain the situation clearly and calmly and attempt to reach an agreement between you. Misunderstanding can arise over simple things and lack of understanding of each other's concerns. It may help to use the college accommodation service as an intermediary, particularly if both parties met via the service.

● In the event of a serious dispute, use a legal service. The NUS will offer advice and your local student union will have some legal contacts. It's unlikely to cost you more than around £5 via Legal Aid even if it isn't a free service, as some colleges provide.

● Disputes which necessitate a recourse to law are not common in lodgings-type accommodation. Welfare and accommodation staff can be particularly helpful in such a dispute.

● If you are unhappy and uncertain what to do, a counsellor may well be a very useful first port-of-call. So often accommodation concerns are interwoven with other concerns, which confuse any working out of solutions.

● If you've a minor complaint eg about the absence of piece of kitchen equipment, and you've not been able to resolve it satisfactorily, the college accommodation office usually issue guidelines to landlords and tenants. A copy of them may suffice to back your case. Just ask the accommodation office if they are prepared to intervene.

CHECKLIST: RATE YOUR ACCOMMODATION

Rate a property, using these 10 factors, on a scale of 1 to 3, in the space provided.

1 = Good/best/unlikely to find better
2 = Adequate/average
3 = Poor/inadequate/expensive

1. The reputation of the area, street, landlord, house, block, flats. How is it rated for fairness of rents, treatment by the landlord or agents, safety of the area, etc?

2. Distance from college and the time/cost of travelling to and fro.

3. The state of decoration and repair of the property noting, particularly, damp and comfort of furniture. Check the adequacy of the kitchen and bathroom facilities.

4. The heating system — its effectiveness and cost. Check the meter system for electricity (expensive) or gas (less so). £2 a day for a one bar electric fire equals £14 per week in the winter.

5. The adequacy of the study facilities. Good study facilities should include an adequate desk, a well-lit, heated and ventilated area to work in, bookshelves, desk chair and armchair.

6. See how the costs compare with similar properties/shares. Deposits can vary considerably and can cost you well over £100 per person, not redeemable until you leave the undamaged property.

7. A clear and catch-free legal agreement should exist: note the circumstances in which it can be terminated.

8. Fees for accommodation agencies should be fixed at reasonable rates eg £10 to £20, refundable minus a small administration fee if you decide not to take the property.

9. Calculate your entitlement to housing benefit (term-time) and its effect upon your overall rent.

10. The acceptability of the people whom you'll be living with or near. Someone as a friendly bedsit neighbour is an enormous asset if you're ill, break your foot or need a lift.

DOMESTIC CHORES

Washing and ironing

A grant won't enable you to throw away your clothes when they're dirty or in need of repair. If you drop your clothes in a pile on the floor or in a bag in the corner, there they will remain a-mouldering; they won't, as so frequently at home, reappear magically in your drawer.

Some students go to amazing lengths to overcome the washing problem. One student parcelled up his dirty clothes each week and sent them home. His clean clothes came back by return post. Another brought enough clothes with her to last the whole term, presumably staggering with large suitcases in each direction at the beginning and end of term.

Other students appear to tackle the problem by washing clothes less often — and sometimes people notice!

How to cope

If you are used to everything you wear being dropped into an automatic washing machine and coming back ironed, it is worthwhile learning a few basic skills before you start out on your own.

Washing your own 'smalls' is one skill that's worth learning before you come away so that you can hand wash them in a sink and dry them on a radiator or near a fire in your room. Using an iron is another skill worth acquiring for those occasions when even your crease resistant or drip dry clothes look too crumpled to wear.

If you are in lodgings, you may find that your landlady will be prepared to wash your clothes for a small fee and, indeed, sometimes for free. In halls of residence or other self-catering accommodation you'll certainly have to wash your own.

Using self-service launderettes

Find out where the local launderette is located and check it against the Students Union's own facilities. Some local launderettes also provide a washing service where, for a very small charge, clothes left at the beginning of the day can be collected at the end.

You may find it helps to get into a regular pattern of taking your washing to the launderette on a particular day of the week. Take with you a pile of appropriate coins (usually 50p, 20p and 10p) and some washing powder. You can buy small packets there but it's cheaper to carry your own in a plastic bag to avoid spillage. Instructions on the wall or other customers will tell you what to do. The launderette's large driers will ensure you go home with dry clothes.

4
Feeding yourself

COOKING, EATING AND DRINKING

The typical student diet

Students in lodgings will normally get a good range and quantity of food, enough for an adequate diet. So, too, will students in halls of residence where food is laid on in refectories, if they choose to eat it. Those who are self-catering, however, may neglect eating and cooking. Shortage of time and lack of know-how are two common reasons.

As a result, a typical self-catering student's diet can leave a lot to be desired. A day may consist of:

No Breakfast
10-11 a.m. Coffee and Mars bar
Lunch — Booze and pasty/pasty and chips
Evening meal — open a tin or two of something-on-toast, *or* same as lunch, *or* call in to the take-away during the night out boozing.

This picture is a generalisation and exaggeration but it reflects the fact that many students neglect eating and cooking. Indeed, a recent biochemistry experiment suggests that many students are found to be deficient in Vitamin C. A lack of Vitamin C leads to a drop in vitality and may lead to a greater susceptibility to infection. Fruit and fresh fruit drinks are a good source of Vitamin C.

For those who want to learn to shop for, cook and eat cheap, quick, nutritious and simple food, the following suggestions will help.

What to eat

Perishables

Bread: Wholemeal bread is more nutritious and better value if
                a bit more expensive.

Eggs: Cheaper in spring and summer. Size 4 is usually big
                enough (Size 1 is biggest).

Milk: Skimmed milk is a bit dearer but better for you.

Yoghurt: You can use plain yoghurt in cooking stirred into a dish
                at the last moment as it cools as a cheaper substitute for
                cream.

Margarine: Sunflower-based margarine is a little more expensive but
                low in polyunsaturates.

Fish: The best fish to buy vary according to the season. The
                cheaper ones include coley and whiting, sprats and
                mackerel.

Meat: Some cheaper cuts are mince, kidneys, liver, belly pork.

Poultry: Chicken and turkey can often be bought in cheap forms,
                eg drumsticks.

Fruit: Important for vitamins but can be expensive so best to
                buy in season, eg grapes, apples, pears are cheaper in
                September/October; oranges and grapefruit are cheaper
                in winter; soft fruits cheaper in June/July.

Vegetables: Important for vitamins but avoid overcooking. Again
                they vary a lot in price according to the season, eg leeks,
                cabbage, cauliflower and root vegetables are cheaper in
                winter; courgettes and beans are cheaper in spring and
                summer.

Salads

There are a vast range of ingredients you can put in a salad and they certainly don't have to be limp-lettuce-and-cucumber rabbit's food.

Among the ingredients that are now in common use, apart from lettuce and cucumber, are tomatoes, onions, radishes and watercress. You
can add washed and chopped vegetables like mushrooms, cabbage, car-
rots and celery. You can add nuts, raisins and chopped fresh fruits. You
can add chopped egg or cheese, grated or cubed.

Further, a salad base, to which some of these ingredients can be added,
can be made with pasta, cold rice or potatoes. You can either cook them
separately and allow them to go cold or use left overs from a hot meal
the previous day.

You can add a simple dressing to these salads, eg yoghurt and lemon
juice or mayonnaise.

Drinks
Coffee and tea can be good for keeping you alert, but too much can have a counter-productive effect. Too much caffeine can cause edginess and depression.

Herb teas are a good alternative. They are beneficial and soothing to the system.

Fruit juices are a source of Vitamin C and provide a refreshing and nutritious drink.

Milk drinks can provide a soothing drink and a certain amount of nutrition. Their problem is that they also provide a high fat content, which is unhealthy.

Basic foods for your store cupboard
The following list of basic foods highlights some useful main meal items (beans, cereals, dried fruit, nuts, pasta, rice and tins) and lists a number of others which are also useful.

Dried beans:	Red, white and green, eg soya and mung beans, chick peas.
Cereals:	Muesli (you can make up your own from oats, dried fruit and nuts).
Dried fruit:	Apricots, apples, prunes, currants, raisins, sultanas.
Nuts:	Brazil nuts, peanuts, broken cashews (the cheapest way to buy them).
Pasta:	Spaghetti, macaroni, lasagne and other forms, also available in wholemeal form.
Rice:	Brown or white — long grain (for savoury food) or short grain (for sweets). Brown rice takes longer to cook but tastes better and is healthier.
Tins:	Tinned foods tend to be expensive and unhealthy ie the E additives (*see* the tin label). However, a few good basics are baked beans, soups, tomatoes and tuna fish.

Other useful items are dates, flour (self-raising and plain), honey, jams, lentils, Marmite, oats, oil (soya and sunflower), sauces (brown, soya, tomato and Worcester), sugar (brown, castor, granulated), vinegar (cider, malt, wine).

Spices and herbs
Useful *spices* include chilli, cinnamon, cloves, coriander, cumin, ginger, nutmeg, paprika, pepper (black, white and cayenne), salt (seasalt). Ready-made mixtures of spices include curry powder, garam masala and tandoori.

Useful *herbs* include basil, bay leaves, marjoram, mint*, parsley*, rosemary*, sage*, thyme*. (Note those marked with an asterisk are easy to grow fresh from seed if you have a space for some pots.) Mixed herbs are also available and can be used with most dishes.

Sesame and sunflower seeds are also useful in your cooking.

Basic equipment
The following would be adequate, basic equipment for your kitchen:

— 2 or 3 saucepans (preferably stainless steel)
— 1 large frying pan or wok
— 1 casserole dish
— 1 large measuring jug
— 1 large wooden spoon
— 1 good sharp knife
— 1 colander
— 1 grater
— 1 pudding dish

Where to shop for food
Most students shop in supermarkets or a convenient local shop. You can buy small quantities of food very easily in supermarkets and they *are* cheaper, but only if you don't buy those items you didn't intend to buy. A shopping list will cut your costs.

Markets are usually much cheaper for fresh fruit and vegetables. Sometimes you can pick them up even cheaper at the end of the day, particularly on Saturdays.

Methods of cooking
There are many methods of cooking. These five main methods are simple and require only one cooking ring and a grill or oven.

1. *Boiling*
Boiling is easy and straightforward, although foods like vegetables can easily lose their taste and nutritional value by overboiling. Five to ten minutes boiling time is adequate for many chopped vegetables.

Boiling is the basic method for cooking pasta, rice, lentils and dried peas.

You can make *a complete meal* by adding ingredients to the same pan in which you have boiled one of these ingredients. *An example meal* would be:

> Boil some pasta and drain off water. Add to the pasta a small knob of margarine, some milk or yoghurt, a tin of tomatoes and some grated cheese. Reheat gently until it is warm enough to eat and you have a complete meal.

"That's funny, it doesn't say how long to boil these sausages for."

2. *Stir-frying*

This is a quick, easy and nutritious method. Use a large pan, a wok or metal casserole dish. Put oil in the pan and when it's hot, add different vegetables, chopped up finely. You can add to these, if you wish, pieces of meat or fish and herbs or spices.

An example for a quick and easy summer dish would be:

> Fry chopped onion and herbs; add tomatoes, courgettes, a tin of tuna fish and lemon juice. Cook for 10 minutes. This can be served with pasta or rice.

You can also use stir-frying as the basis for *soup* by adding to the cooked vegetables a pint or so of liquid (water or vegetable juices). If you wish you can add a large spoon of Marmite or a stock cube as well.

3. *Baking*

You can bake things in an oven very easily by putting all the ingredients into one dish with sufficient liquid to keep it moist.

For example fish can be cooked this way by adding a little margarine or butter and milk.

4. *Grilling*

You can cook fish, poultry and several cuts of meat (ask what's suitable for grilling) by putting them under the grill on a low heat and grilling slowly. Also, this is a useful method for snacks such as cheese and tomato on toast.

5. *Steaming*

Steaming food has long been popular by using *pressure cookers*. For under £20 you can buy a pressure cooker to use on gas or electric cookers, which will cook food quickly without loosing much of its quality. You can also buy *steamers* for use over open pans, which will cook several vegetables in tiers, at the same time, without losing their nutritional value.

Some other hints on cooking

Before you go to college you could make a list of the things you can cook. *If* you have a list (!) work your way through it, developing your confidence by concentrating initially on those things you know how to do eg boiling an egg.

Even if you only know one dish which you feel you can cook — spaghetti bolognese or macaroni cheese — you can feed yourself for a while. After the seventh night you may need a change, which is where using the friends who share the accommodation can help. If each of you has one or two specialisms you can keep each other going for a while until your expertise expands a bit.

Some friends, or couples living together, invest in a *microwave oven* for speed and cheapness of cooking (after an initial three figure investment). You can certainly produce food very quickly following the microwave cookbook provided when you buy one. It's not idiot proof, but it certainly provides a chance to try simple cooking methods which will aid your survival.

Alternatively, if you've decided the whole cooking venture is beyond you at this stage, you will need the luck of finding a friend who *can* cook and who *wants* to cook for you.

Included in the section on 'Useful Reading' at the back of the book are some good simple guides to cooking.

Take-aways and eating out

Take-aways are used by students a great deal. Restaurants are used less frequently as they are usually beyond most students' pockets.

Neither take-away food nor restaurant food represents good value for money compared with eating at home in the way described here. The take-away food industry has boomed because it makes good profits, which is not good value to students. Which take-away foods you prefer is a matter of taste but excessive eating of fat-based foods such as chips, sausages, hamburgers and pasties is not likely to supply you with a good diet and may well have an ill-effect on your energy, health and concentration.

Jacket potatoes with fillings are often the best of the take-away bunch, although very cheap and easy to cook for yourself in the oven at home for an hour or so at one fifth of the cost. A shared meal with friends in a carefully selected Chinese restaurant can still represent good value too. Arts centres frequently provide cheap, nutritious food.

Snacking

A snack can be cheap, quick and provide a nourishing meal. Two good examples are sandwiches and soup with bread.

A wholemeal bread cheese *sandwich* with lettuce and tomato, add to this an apple or yoghurt, and you have a well-balanced, sustaining meal.

Tinned *soup* with a slice of wholemeal bread can make a substantial and satisfying snack. Whilst the additives in tins like these may be a disadvantage, you can make soups easily yourself — *see* the section on Stir-frying on p37.

5
Stretching the cash

Grants have fallen in value

According to the NUS the necessities of life, accommodation and food, absorb an increasingly large proportion of your grant. In a 1984 NUS report '*Undergraduate Income and Expenditure*' there were estimates that 60-65% of grants were spent on necessities. In 1987 some NUS staff estimate the figure was 80%. Grants have fallen in real value.

Most students still receive some form of grant, although the 98% of 1984 may now be a lower percentage. Some awards only cover fees. A grant topped up by parental contribution and covenanted income represents the main source of cash for the majority of students in higher education. The inadequacy of the grant is emphasised by the parents who fail to pay their off-spring their full contribution. 25% of students are estimated to be disadvantaged by the failure of parents to pay their full contribution.

The implication of these trends is that there is a pressure upon you to manage your money effectively, which is why this chapter considers:

- Possible additional grants
- Managing income and expenditure
- Do's and dont's of budgeting cash
- Finding help in cash emergencies
- Earning in term time
- Claiming state benefits
- Where to keep your money

In addition to your assessed grant entitlement, topped up with parental contribution or covenant, you should check your entitlement to additional grants.

Check your entitlement to additional grants

● *Purchase of special equipment.* The costs can be very high on certain courses eg fashion or design courses. In some cases these can amount to £500 or more over your college life. Discuss this with your college and LEA before the course starts if possible and find out what help is available.

● *For extra weeks' attendance.* The LEA will pay you for each additional week you have to attend your course beyond 30 weeks and 3 days. Amount varies but will be £5 or more per day.

● *For vacation study.* If you attend an academic course in the vacation at the recommendation of your college, you are advised to claim a daily rate attendance payment.

● *For disability.* As a disabled student, you can claim an allowance of around £600 if you can demonstrate expenditure you have incurred.

● *For field work trips.* Residential field work trips may be eligible for LEA support but it is very difficult to obtain.

● *For travel.* Although Scottish students can claim travel costs over a certain limit (£50 in 1987), most students can't now claim travel expenses separately. There are some exceptions, for instance those vocationally training in fields such as medicine and social work.

● *For study overseas.* If your course involves an overseas placement, you are entitled to at least the London area grant rate. Check with your LEA.

"Oh dear, no money in the food jar again."

Working out your income and expenditure

You can use the checklist (below) to work out your weekly budget, adding any other category of income or expenditure missing from the list. Used in conjunction with the **Tips for budgeting your cash** on the next page you'll have more chance of surviving financially.

Your income	£ per term	Your expenditure	£ per week
One term's grant (actual amount):	_____	Rent:	_____
Parental contribution (if any):	_____	Food and non-alcoholic drink:	_____
Earnings from vacation or part-time job (if any):	_____	Bills (heating, lighting, HP, etc.):	_____
		Laundry and cleaning:	_____
Other cash (if any):	_____	Transport and travel:	_____
Interim total =	_____	Phone, stationery, papers, magazines:	_____
Subtract from this any sums to be set aside for the vacation, treats, presents, clothes, shoes and emergencies:	_____	Books:	_____
		Entertainment (include nights out, sport, hobbies, etc.):	_____
Final total =	_____		
Divide by the number of weeks in the in the term to find weekly income (eg £550 ÷ 11 = £50 pw):		Other: e.g. repairs, insurance	_____
			_____
TOTAL PER WEEK	_____	TOTAL PER WEEK	_____

Tips for budgeting your cash

DO

- Plan a notional budget for each week. Note the likely arrival times of grant, parental payments and covenanted money, allowing for holidays as well as term time.

- Have a system for paying for rent and fuel that ensures you protect this money for essentials.

- Keep a running total of cash spent. A weekly check will help you monitor out-goings, noting expenditure on a bank statement or in a notebook.

- Ask parents or guardians to pay their contributions by regular payments rather than one large sum which is more difficult to manage. This could be achieved by standing order payments direct to your bank account.

- Put some money aside for special purchases e.g. a piece of equipment needed for your course; a special present for a family member; Christmas; repairing your bike or hifi.

- Keep any large cash sum you may be drawing upon in a deposit account, where it will earn interest. You can arrange for regular sums to be paid from it into your current account, which will structure your expenditure.

- Allow for short-term cash problems at the beginning and end of terms. It is at these times that cash may fail to arrive or run out, respectively. Have an emergency arrangement set up or, preferably, some standby cash nest-egg available.

DON'T

- Spend a lot of money before you arrive at college. You're more likely to need it when you're there. This particularly applies to spending money on expensive textbooks before you know they are really needed.

- Use plastic money on a regular basis if you're inexperienced at handling cards like Visa and Access. Enormous debt problems with cards are an increasing feature of students' cash crises. You'll also pay out a fortune in interest charges, wasting your money and increasing your debts.

● Purchase expensive consumer goods early in the year or term. A few hundred pounds spent in one lump sum, without adequate financial back up, will leave you struggling throughout the term, the year — even the course.

● Spend freely on eating out, drinking and social life at the beginning of term, until you've established a pattern of balanced weekly expenditure. It is tempting to do so if you've cast yourself in the role of the generous extrovert or are concerned about missing out on any of the night life.

● Scrimp on insuring your valuables in an effort to save cash. Theft is common on campuses and in some types of accommodation used by students. Bikes, bags, cameras and electrical equipment are targets. You can obtain policies geared to students from your SU office: Endsleigh Insurance Services are linked to the NUS.

Where to turn when you've run out of cash

When you have run out of money or plunged yourself into debt, it is often difficult to face the crisis. Running away can feel attractive as a solution but the best survival routes lie in facing key people who may be able to help. Hopefully you will be able to rescue the situation, over time, but it is important to realise that cash problems are among the most difficult to resolve easily.

● Speak to your *bank*. Make an appointment and discuss your debt problems face-to-face. Try to get an appointment with the member of staff who deals with student problems. Ask what you'll have to do to get out of debt and what credit will be made available to you — and when. Even if they refuse to help, you'll know where you stand.

● Speak to your *SU Welfare Officer*. Ask about the possibility of short-term emergency loans from any SU or College Trust Fund. Amounts of up to £100 may be available, if certain conditions are met.

● Check *Educational Charities* to see if you can apply for a one-off cash payment to help you rescue your finances. Useful books are listed on p.46, and you'll find them at the SU or Careers Information room. However you'll have to wait for your application to be considered. Several months will normally elapse, so this won't help in the short-term.

● Speak to key approachable members of *your family*. Reluctant though you may be to both inform them and ask them for help, specific family members can act as useful sounding boards.

● Speak to a *Counsellor* to help you cope with the worry and sort out your thoughts on what to do and who to see.

● Approach *specialist agencies.* Try the *Citizens' Advice Bureau (CAB)* where specialist help may be available called debt counselling. If you have dependants, you may be eligible for the *DHSS Hardship Scheme.* Check with the *NUS Welfare Manual* as to your possible eligibility before contacting the DHSS. The *LEA* may respond to your vacation hardship, if you apply for a *Vacation Hardship Allowance.* Check your eligibility with your SU, welfare office or CAB.

Sources of cash

1. *Borrowing*
A common route but mined with practical and relationship problems. You risk guilt, breaking trust and loss of independence and credibility if you borrow from family or friends. You are still stuck with the repayment problem as well.

2. *Sell something*
Any more valuable possession can be considered in dire circumstances — the bike, your hifi, some collector's piece . . .

3. *Earn some cash*
Piling in the hours on some part-time job at weekends or nights may help temporarily alleviate the crisis. The obvious problems are tiredness, the effect upon studying and social life. See the part-time job ideas list (p.47).

4. *Apply to trust and charities*
As previously explained, a medium term rather than short-term strategy.

5. *Pawn something*
Some larger towns and cities still have pawn shops where you can leave some valuables in return for cash and a ticket with which to redeem the article — once you return the cash.

Warning
Avoid *loan agencies,* specialising in unsecured loans and charging very high and punitive interest rates. Interest quickly accumulates and becomes very difficult to pay back.

Useful reading
NUS Welfare Manual, Educational Charities, Charities Digest, How to Claim State Benefits.

Two main ways to earn money
You can earn money during term time by seeking part-time employment during the day. Many jobs are available in the evenings, overnight or at weekends. Alternatively, you can use your own enterprise and skills to obtain cash.

1. Part-time employment
There are several main types of employment.

● *Hotel and catering work*
Work in pubs (try your own SU first), bars, clubs, wine bars, hotels, restaurants and fast food outlets. Typical tasks are serving customers, washing up and cleaning and preparing food.

● *Shop work*
Sales assistant work, shelf stacking or cashier work in supermarkets, fashion chain stores, department stores and the like on Saturdays or day-time shifts.

● *Work as an interviewer/researcher*
Work for diverse organisations involved in market research for commercial agencies, opinion polls, broadcasting.

● *Overnight work*
Petrol stations, residential homes and mini-cab offices are examples.

● *Work for local authority services*
This can involve such diverse activities as being a nude model for a still-life drawing class to working as a lifeguard (assuming you can save people) at the local swimming pool.

2. Using your own enterprise and skills
Some paid employment involves using your own skills and initiative but the suggestions below are examples of job creation that are possible when you are seeking cash for survival — or enriching life.

● *Using training from previous courses and experience from previous jobs*
Examples are upholstering furniture, typing dissertations and projects, nursing, child care and youth work.

● *Seeking outlets for your creative skills, which could include*
Playing guitar in a local pub; busking at a regular — profitable — town centre pitch; selling your paintings, pots or craft work to local craft shops; selling your jewellery at local craft markets; decorating cakes to order for special occasions; setting up your own small item removal business with an old van; coaching in a sport or recreational activity eg a particular musical instrument or a form of martial art.

Where to keep your money
You have a choice of main types of account in which to keep your money
— banks, building societies, National Girobank.

Which bank?
The answer to this question may be none of them if you've a flexible
building society account. Most students do open a bank account by their
first year in college and the big clearing banks certainly make bids for
the student accounts. They do so as they know you're likely to be professional, and profitable, customers in future years. Further, they know that
in Britain, most customers don't change their bank once they've opened
an account.

● Choosing the 'best buy' bank for you in any one year may involve
  weighing up the different starting offers. *Which?* magazine helps with
  this process, running occasional analyses of the most attractive offers.
  However, starting offers are only one way of making the judgement.

● It's worth checking what bank charges will be made *after* you cease
  to be a student; some banks increase charges considerably.

● The proximity of a bank to the college is another important criterion.
  A campus bank can make life easier, but check their opening hours.

● If you're with another bank, check to see if they'll charge you for
  cashing a cheque.

Overdrafts
According to the NUS most students have bank accounts and the majority (56 per cent) have overdrafts at some stage in their course. Most
students managed to keep the overdraft to under £100 or so but 1 in 10
in the NUS Report (1984) had overdrafts which had reached £200 and
a few individuals had overdrafts of £1,000 or more.

The problem with overdrafts is that they don't go away. Money over-
spent one term is paid back out of the following term's grant. As a result
you find you have less money for that term and need another overdraft
and so on. On top of this, interest is charged on the amount overdrawn
so you have even less money to start the following term.

Building Societies
Many building societies now have cheque books, cheque and cash cards,
with accompanying machines. Interest is paid on the small sums that are
likely to lie there: no overdrafts are allowed. The latter could be a real
advantage.

National Girobank

Well worth considering as it has all the usual cheque book, cheque guarantee card, cash machine card (for the 'Link' machines) and paying in services. Convenient hours with the use of local post offices are other features.

Finally you may wish to compare these services with your old *National Savings Ordinary Account* and your little blue book you've trotted up to the Post Office with for all the years of your youth. The extra facilities of the others certainly encourage you to spend more.

Supplementary benefit

Your grant will include an element of cash help for tiding you over the Christmas and Easter vacations. For that reason, the majority of students will be unable to claim any state benefit, called supplementary benefit, if they are unemployed over these two vacations. As you are not seen as being available for work as a full-time student, you cannot claim supplementary benefit during term-time either.

If you are unemployed in the summer vacation, you are often able to claim supplementary benefit. You need to claim by form B1 from an unemployment benefit office and leaflet SB 21 explains all. Another useful DHSS booklet is FB 23 *Going to College or University? A pocket guide to social security,* available from your local DHSS office.

Check your entitlement by calling at your local office and joining the queue. Allow some time for your visit as these queues can be slow moving, as can the Girocheque which will arrive if your claim is successful. Delays of two weeks or so before your first payment are routine and four to six weeks quite common, so don't rely on it for the first weeks of the summer.

"Can I claim Supplementary Benefit for the dogs?"

6
Body maintenance

Keeping healthy

Studying is largely a passive activity. Hours are spent at desks, in lecture theatres, armchairs — and beds. You have the freedom to lose sleep, prop up bars, eat junk food and, generally, physically neglect yourself. This chapter focuses upon what you can do to look after yourself both by using medical services and by self-help. Some self-help can start before you get to college.

Before you go to college

Looking after yourself at college can start before you leave home. Planning some nutritious food to cook yourself or the sport and recreation you'll take part in are two good examples.

It is also advisable for you to bring with you, if living away at college, your *medical card,* having completed any *medical enquiry form* the college might have sent you. *Inform* the college and/or landlady in advance of any special *health or dietary needs* you have. A booster or primary *tetanus jab* would be especially useful if you are in contact with soil as part of your college life, eg in active sports, climbing and potholing, or in studying courses such as botany, archaeology, environmental science and geology.

Registering with a doctor

Registering with a doctor whilst away from home is advisable and does not prevent you receiving treatment in the vacations from your doctor at home. Register early before the November or February viruses strike, otherwise you may find yourself with a long delay in receiving help as a result of not registering. Many colleges have their own medical service, with a doctor and nursing staff, and a large proportion of students register with such a service.

It is important to check the hours that any doctor is available to see you so that you spot any clashes with your timetable. If you aren't able to visit the college doctor at surgery times, it may be better to register with another practice close to your accommodation. This is a point particularly relevant to those students who are heavily time-tabled on intensive courses, eg many engineering students.

Medical services for students

Although not all colleges have a general practitioner (GP) service available to students, nearly all have a nurse, nursing officer or matron. In addition, a first aid system will operate in the college as a backup to the nurse in the case of accident and emergency.

Nursing services tend to be very well used. If you are in doubt whether to call to see a doctor or counsellor, the nurse would be an appropriate person from whom to seek advice. You can receive help with vaccinations and injections and first aid treatment. A contraceptive service for females will also usually be available where a GP is in attendance.

Prescriptions are free for students and other services are at low cost for low-income students. (It is your income, not your parents, which is taken into account in calculating your entitlement.) Thus dental charges and National Health Service spectacles may well be at lower prices.

What do students visit doctors for?

Students use doctors for a wide range of reasons. In general, however, you are a healthier group of the population in terms of major illness and ill-health. You are, however, often coping with the stresses of student life, caring for yourself for the first time and coping with your own personal and sexual development. As a result, many female students visit the doctor for contraceptive advice, with concerns over periods or urinary infections. Stomach and headache complaints are common to both sexes as are the usual batch of virus infections such as flu and coughs.

But many doctors feel that some physical symptoms reflect emotional stress. Loneliness, difficulty in coping with study deadlines, exams or personal relationships are common sources of stress. Disabling anxiety and depression are not uncommon among students. Some doctors will not automatically offer you pills if you're experiencing such stress. They may offer to listen. Others, seeing your need, may suggest you see a counsellor for the same listening help.

If you become ill

If you become ill, ensure you have informed someone who can be of reliable help to you. A friend can call a doctor, let your tutor know of your ill health and pass messages and requests for help to key people if you are unable to visit a doctor personally. Don't allow yourself to be isolated. Let your family know, too, as they may well be concerned if they haven't heard from you.

You are allowed up to two weeks ill-health without having to notify your tutor formally in most colleges, four weeks before the LEA has to be informed.

Good reasons for active exercise

There are several good reasons for participating in active physical activity whilst at college.

1. Effective study is aided by a feeling of physical well-being. Illness, being overweight, unfitness and tiredness are likely to sap your energy and concentration upon studying.

2. It provides opportunities for meeting a wide cross-section of students from outside your course. It can also involve travel and visiting places and people in other parts of Britain and the world, for example skiing in France, climbing in the Highlands, surfing at Newquay or athletic competition in Budapest.

3. It will help you fend off anxiety, depression and loneliness.

4. It is a useful, sometimes even essential selling point to prospective employers, who look for evidence of the 'all-rounder' who has used time at college to the full and has demonstrated an ability to function in groups. Thus an Oxbridge blue, a place in a sports team, a position of responsibility as captain/vice captain or the membership of a committee can all be indicators of a potentially resourceful employee.

5. There's a vast range of choice — probably more than you've ever had before. Clubs and societies offering marvellous — and cheap — opportunities for activity, excitement, challenge and fun.

CHECKLIST: LOOK AFTER YOURSELF

- Look around for individual or team activities to help you keep, or get, fit and to supply the necessary oxygen to your brain.

- Check your diet and try to keep it in balance. Supplementing the guidelines in Chapter 4 with items like Vitamin C tablets to ward off winter coughs and sneezes.

- Watch what you drink. Alcohol is still the major drug problem in most colleges. Excessive caffeine consumption, particularly in the form of coffee, can be harmful to composed studying.

- Monitor over-indulgence. Student life involves the opportunity to sample those aspects of life which may have been previously denied. It's easy to go over the top.

- Consider learning techniques of self-protection. Examples are women's self-defence groups, judo and karate, all of which may increase your confidence in the face of threat.

- Be aware of peer group pressure to join in the drugs scene. It can be an easy cop-out to facing your real emotional needs for success, friendships, ease of talking to people and sexual relationships.

- Check you're meeting your needs for sleep.

- Watch your personal hygiene and sexual behaviour. It's not just AIDS you face by risky, unprotected sexual relationships: there are other sexual diseases and skin and urinary troubles.

7
Cheap travel and transport

Costly travel

Travel to and from college can be a very expensive business. Even if you live at home, travel costs can be high if, for example, you are involved in using your own transport to travel twenty miles each day or are crossing London by public transport. If you are living away from home, a travel allowance is incorporated into your grant so you are unable to claim additional money from the LEA to cover your journeys to and from home. The exception to this is if you are receiving a grant from the Scottish Education Department, when expenditure of over £50 may be reclaimed provided you are following the required regulations.

Local transport

The cost of public transport can vary in cost enormously from one area of the country to another. So, too, can the availability and regularity of bus services. Thus, checking the costs, routes and convenience of buses to and from your key locations is a vital step to take before committing yourself to some particular accommodation. It's no joke to be six miles from college on an irregular and costly bus route with the last bus leaving town at 10.30 pm. It destroys social life and fosters isolation.

If you have your own transport with you at college you are likely to have more freedom but problems can still occur. Although parking is unlikely to be a problem for bikes, pedal bikes are a particular target for theft, so a good locking system is advisable. Finding your way around by bike or car can also lead to a number of problems in the early days, eg driving the wrong way up one-way streets.

The cheapest forms of travel

Walking, biking, picking up a lift with a friend and hitching remain the cheapest forms of transport. *Walking* isn't usually feasible for longer journeys. *Bikes,* too, have a limited range for journeys you'd like to complete in a day or so.

Lifts are a feasible way of getting around the country. You may well find lifts via the informal network of your college. Your contacts with other course members can produce lifts, as can notices on SU noticeboards or in SU papers.

Hitching is still popular, both in Britain and in other countries in which it is permitted. Although vast numbers of people hitch each year, carrying their destination cards and using the tips for pick-up points passed on by other hitchers, there are problems involved in hitching.

Every year there are reminders of the risk element in hitching. Sexual assault, rape, violence and even death affect a small minority of those who hitch. If you are planning to hitch and are inexperienced, use the guidelines of those who know the ropes and, preferably, travel in pairs.

Your own car at college

It is expensive to run even the oldest of bangers. Students frequently have problems with cars for, apart from the probable breakdowns, other cash problems can occur. Failing to find the money to pay road tax or insurance on time or to repair the silencer and change the worn tyres bring students into conflict with the law as well as the bank manager.

Parking is often a problem too. In city centre colleges it is often more difficult than on a campus college. Where student car parks exist, they are frequently jammed with cars with the consequent difficulty of getting out once you've got in. Word of mouth usually informs you of the best local streets in which to park.

You'll be faced with fewer problems at a campus college, where parking is (normally) less hassle.

Launching out

There are numerous opportunities for travel by coach, rail, boat and plane, with discounts and special packages for students. See p.58 for where to get tickets.

Coach

Coach travel has increased its share of the student travel market substantially in the 80s. The best coach transport is cheap, fast and comfortable with a toilet, video equipment and refreshments served on board. You can buy a *Student Coach Card* from your local SU Travel Centre or direct from National Express Ltd, Midland House, 1 Vernon Road, Edgbaston, Birmingham B16 9SJ. It costs £3.50 and entitles you to 33% discounts on standard fares plus other discounts. It is valid for 12 months. You'll find local coach companies will offer student discounts for long-distance travel, as do continental coach travel firms such as Euroways and Supabus.

Rail

Rail travel is still very popular with students who live long distances from their college and find faster and more direct routes home than coach travel provides — dependent on where you live and the networks that exist.

Buy a *British Rail Young Persons Rail Card* for 12 months, saving 33% on 'saver' fares. It costs £12 and is available for those under 24 and/or in full-time further education. The *Inter-Rail Card* gives you unlimited European travel for 1 month for £139. To be eligible you must be under 26 or in full-time further education. *Transalpino Ltd*, 71-75 Buckingham Palace Road, London SW1 (01-834 9656 or 6283), offer rail travel, with around half-price fares for those under 26, whether students or not. Students over 26 are not eligible for their cheap tickets, which cover most of Europe and some other countries as well and are valid for 2 months. Book in advance at peak times, by telephone if you are using a credit card.

You'll need to prove your age by quoting your passport number. Show your driving licence or passport/passport number if booking in person, or if a relative or friend is booking for you.

Boat

Price reductions on boats are less generous than other forms of transport. Some exceptions are Sealink and B & I which offer discounts if you have an *Inter-Rail Card*. Townsend Thoresen and Hoverspeed offer one-third off normal fares on many routes.

You may be able to travel cheaply by a *merchant cargo boat* from some selected ports to European destinations, particularly if you have contacts with shipping employees. If you're an experienced sailor, you could hawk your services around local marinas or yacht clubs as *crew* for another way of cheap boat travel.

Air

Ask at your local student travel office about the various types of reductions available for specific destinations. Discounts vary according to destination, time of year and type of ticket. You can find a 25% reduction on a 'student' or 'youth' booking on a *normal flight. Standby tickets* can be bought at your travel centre or at the airport on the departure day, if they are available: they are not always available for all flights. They are cheap but you may have long airport waits at peak times of year and/or popular routes. *Advance Purchase Excursion (APEX)* fares are widely available and much cheaper than normal fares. Disadvantages are that you have to book at least a month in advance and have fixed departure and return dates with heavy penalties for changing them ie you can lose all your money.

The Student Air Travel Association operate student *charter flights* to the USA, Israel and Europe. Good value tickets, valid for 6 months and more flexible than APEX.

Finding out more about travel

There are several key resources.

● Your *SU Student Travel Centre*
Most colleges have a travel centre which will sell tickets for most of the discount travel schemes mentioned in this chapter. They'll also sell you Endsleigh (NUS) or ISIS insurance packages for your travel. You'll most probably find you'll need an ISIC card (see below).

● Two useful travel agencies: Student Travel Centre, Tours and Travel (STCTT), 18 Rupert Street, London W1 (01-434 1306), and London Student Travel, 52 Grosvenor Gardens, London SW1 (01-730 8111).

● Buy an *International Student Identity Card (ISIC)* from your travel centre or from NUS Marketing, PO Box 190, London, WC1 (01-272 9445). Send £3.50 with proof you're a student and a large sae. With it you'll get an International Student Travel Guide listing discounts and benefits in the UK and abroad.

● For cheap air flights it may be worth checking *'bucket shops'*, as they are known, ie shops which specialise in selling cheap air tickets off-loaded quietly to them by major airlines with spare seating. They, and standby tickets, are often the cheapest. Find someone who has bought from a bucket shop before and who knows the ropes, being very careful to check the flight conditions.

● Check schemes like *BUNAC* and *Camp America* (see next chapter) for cheap or paid-for flights to the USA in return for a summer job in a children's camp.

Useful Reading

Europe: a manual for hitchikers (Vacation Work Publications)
Europe by Train (Fontana)
Travel Survival Kit series (Vacation Work Publications)

8
Varied vacations

How many holiday weeks?
One of the main features of higher education for students on full-time courses is the extensive vacations.

In a typical school year you'd get 13 weeks or so of holiday. The table (below) shows how many extra weeks you'll get in higher eduation.

TYPE OF INSTITUTION	MAXIMUM WEEKS PER TERM	WEEKS IN ACADEMIC YEAR	MINIMUM VACATION WEEKS
Polytechnics and CHEs	11	33	19
Most university courses	10	30	22
Oxbridge	8	24	28

In reality, you may find yourself with even more time at your disposal as many courses effectively finish immediately after examinations eg mid-June, so you may end up with a couple of weeks in which to recuperate before the official end of the academic year.

Typically the vacation weeks are divided thus:

- Christmas Vacation 4/5 weeks
- Easter Vacation   4/5 weeks
- Summer Vacation   10 plus weeks

Exceptions include *sandwich* courses, particular 'thin' sandwich courses where 3 to 6 month periods away from college are spent in employment or further training. However such sandwich work is paid, with the advantages that entails. *Field work* courses can also occupy weeks of Easter and Summer vacations in courses as wide apart as geology and languages.

Choices in vacations

For many students the vacations, particularly the summer vacation, present a series of choices and the need to balance time and energy spent in the family home, on social life and travel, or in earning money.

Many students compromise spending some time at home, some time earning money and then travelling. Many combine two of these needs by, for example, working abroad or earning some cash whilst living at home. There are things to do that don't involve paid work, as well.

The main choices

There are several alternatives which offer scope for a well-used vacation.

● *A stay at home* can give you the chance to rest and relax, catching up on important relationships with family and friends.

● *Travel* may involve visiting college friends on their home territory or setting off alone to far-off places. Friends often use the vac as a chance to team up and visit or holiday in various parts of the world as cheaply as possible. Virtually every part of the world has British students visiting in the summer.

● *Voluntary work* can vary from a few hours a week helping the elderly or handicapped via your local *Council for Voluntary Service* to a major time commitment like the *St George's Community Cultural Project, Liverpool* with its 12 hour day and six day week. You'll find other projects, which like St George's offer some kind of cheap or free accommodation and food deal in return for your labour, by asking about *Community Service Volunteers.* Opportunities exist for work on *archaeological digs* and for conservation work on the environment via organisations like the *British Trust for Conservation Volunteers* (BTCV), a nationwide charitable trust and the UK's largest organisation offering practical projects all the year round.

● *Expeditions* and *special ventures* may include joining a university expedition down a South American river, spending time at a pop festival or on a special social work placement on East-side Manhattan.

● *Summer study* could involve you in international travel. For example, you can go to the USA via the *Council on International Educational Exchange* — at a cost. Organisations like *CRAC* (Careers Research & Advisory Council) run Insight Courses into areas like Management, Management in Retailing and Entrepreneurship to give you taster experiences on the world of work.

Some points to note

● Some of these opportunities can also involve longer periods of time eg an exchange to the USA for a year, or longer volunteer periods *(Voluntary Service Overseas* is 2, preferably 3 years plus).

● There can be conflicts and problems in any of these options, eg rows at home, misery abroad!

● Some ideas involve you laying out cash eg for Camp America you'll need to take £200-£300; USA study can involve over £1,000.

● Interesting use of the vac is a major selling point to future prospective employers.

A job in the vac?

An NUS survey in the 1980s pointed out that vacation employment had become less important as a source of income for students. Less than one in five students work for ten vacation weeks a year as jobs for students reflect the general economic scene and unemployment levels.

Christmas vacation work also occupies about one in five students, many of whom will be working on the post, in shops and restaurants. Many students avoid working in *Easter vacs* because of the imminence of May/June exams. It is the summer vac that is the most important earning time for nearly all students.

HOW TO LIVE & WORK IN AMERICA Steve Mills

The only title available which explains America's rules and regulations on immigration — a world of quotas, permits, 'green cards' and special categories.
160pp, illustrated. £5.95 paperback.   0 7463 0330 0

HOW TO LIVE & WORK IN AUSTRALIA Laura Veltman

Expert advice which meets a long-standing need for inside information on how to become a temporary or permanent Australian resident.
192pp, illustrated. £5.95 paperback.   0 7463 0331 9

WORKING ABROAD? Harry Brown

Completely revised and updated, this new edition of the best-seller *Working Abroad?* meets a real need for information and advice crucial to every expatriate.
160pp, illustrated. £6.95 paperback.   0 7463 0383 1

Northcote House Publishers, Harper & Row House,
Estover Road, Plymouth PL6 7PZ, United Kingdom.
Tel: (0752) 705251. Telex: 45635. FAX: (0752) 777603.

Summer vac jobs

Many summer jobs are low paid, unskilled or semi-skilled manual work. You may also find more interesting opportunities, both home and abroad. Some of the main employments are:

- *Work with children* eg holiday schemes, adventure playgrounds, childminding, au pair, Bunacamp, home help.
- *Work in the holiday and leisure industries* eg holiday camps, caravan parks, lifeguard work, coaching, waiting, cleaning, cooking, shop work.
- *Selling* eg ice cream van sales, 'rep' work, doorstep selling of double glazing and the like.
- *Driving* eg van deliveries, removals work, tractors.
- *Market Research* eg completing questionnaires for a national park about summer usage, work for polling organisations, TV and Radio research.
- *Shop and office work* eg work in 'Next' or 'Marks and Sparks', bank and insurance company work, helping out in local shop or store, work in the accounts office at the local builders.
- *Placement type jobs* eg some chartered accountants offer short 4 week placements for those considering accountancy as a career.
- *Factory work* eg the food industries, particularly confectionary and meat, offer work on the line as summer cover for holidaying employees.
- *Earning from entertainment and art* eg street entertainment, busking, modelling, playing in a band, street painting, film extra, studio work.
- *Fruit and vegetable picking* eg hop picking in Kent, lifting potatoes, picking apples in France, harvesting peas in the north-west USA.

Find out more

- You can find out more by talking to other students and asking how they found out about their vacation opportunities.

- Check your careers information room at college. It will have files and books about every type of vacation experience. You'll find the books listed below there.

Useful Addresses

BAVE (CRAC Australia/New Zealand Travel/Work scheme)
Details of 8 week scheme from your careers information office or CRAC, Bateman Street, Cambridge CB2 1LZ (0223 354551).

BUNAC (British Universities North America Club)
232 Vauxhall Bridge Road, London SW1V 1AU (01-630 0344)
£2 a year membership offers you a US work permit for a USA summer
job and a cheap flight over. Any age student in higher education can apply.
Apply early. Jobs vary from *Bunacamp* summer children's camps to service industry jobs in restaurants, hotels and shops.

Camp America, 37 Queens Gate, London SW7 5HR (01-589 3223/4)

Vacation Work Books, 9 Park End Street, Oxford.

Useful Reading
Summer Jobs Britain, Susan Griffith (Vacation Work) Annual
Summer Jobs Abroad, David Woodworth (Vacation Work) Annual
Summer Employment USA (distributed by Vacation Work)
Emplois D'Été en France (VAC-JOB) Annual
Working in Ski Resorts (Vacation Work)
Working Holidays (Central Bureau for Educational Visits and Exchanges
— CBEVE)
Adventure and Discovery, Hilary Sewell (CBEVE)
Adventure Holidays 1986, Simon Calder (Vacation Books)
Sleep Cheap in Europe (£1.20) includes booking vouchers and tips on cheap
places to stay. From NUS Marketing.
How to Live & Work in America, Steve Mills (Northcote House Publishers
Ltd)
How to Live & Work in Australia, Laura Veltman (Northcote House
Publishers Ltd)
Working Abroad? Harry Brown (Northcote House Publishers Ltd)

How to Pass Exams Without Anxiety
David Acres

Newly available, David Acres' highly-praised book *must* be the first choice for candidates taking examinations at any level. As well as giving really professional guidance on revision and examination techniques, it includes many proven ideas for coping with anxiety, and guidelines for parents and others involved with helping examination candidates. With its quick-reference headings, the text is very clearly laid out and easy to use and will save students hours of precious revision time.
112pp, illustrated. £3.95 paperback.
0 7463 0334 3

Successful Exam Technique
David Cocker

Attractively laid out in self-contained spreads, this remarkably easy-to-use paperback breaks new ground for those thousands of students who want to develop a really winning revision and examination technique. With its quick reference headings, graphics, cartoons, checklists and summaries, it will be the one absolutely essential purchase for examination candidates throught the English-speaking world, who want down-to-earth help and want it fast.
96pp, illustrated. £3.95 paperback.
0 7463 0348 3

How to Use a Library
Elizabeth King

Libraries of all kinds have undergone radical change and improvement in recent years. No longer are they just repositories of books — they have become real 'information supermarkets' offering a vast range of broadly-based services and facilities. This up-to-the-minute handbook shows students and everyone today how to use libraries — not just school, college and public libraries, but "resource centres" of all kinds ranging from specialist collections to major business and official libraries, for study, work and leisure.
96pp, illustrated. £4.95 paperback.
0 7463 0317 0

Northcote House Publishers, Harper & Row House, Estover Road, Plymouth PL6 7PZ, United Kingdom. Tel: (0752) 705251; Telex: 45635; FAX: (0752) 777603

9
Studying and passing exams

INTRODUCTION

There is frequently a big contrast between the study atmosphere at college and the sixth form you've left behind. Even if your 'A' level/OND studying was conducted in a fairly easy-going atmosphere you are likely to find the atmosphere of higher education very different. Although there are some highly structured and fully timetabled courses, and some staff who keep a very close eye on what you're doing and may even badger you, these are the exceptions rather than the rule.

Most of you will find you have hours of time to organise for yourself and that nobody will tell you how to use it. Of the 168 hours in the week, you will have somewhere between 10 and 30 hours of formal course commitment. The rest of the time is for you to use or misuse as you please. Few staff will hassle you for work. If you fail to produce it, that is your responsibility, even if failing to meet a deadline can mean failing some course components, or at an extreme, the year. For in addition to adjusting to the new found freedom, you will be faced with new styles of teaching and assessment.

GET TO KNOW THE SYSTEM

The college prospectus will give you some idea of the structure of your course, the subjects and an outline of the assessment procedure. Once you have your timetable, the reality of a typical week will begin to crystallise. You will begin to see how lectures, tutorials or seminars fit into the week. You'll understand the relative balance between the theoretical and the practical components of the course such as laboratories, workshops and field work. The course-work demands will emerge and deadlines will be set for essays, preparing seminars, worked examples, lab and other reports, reading and project work.

Lectures

Lectures vary a great deal in form and quality and are still a mainstay of college teaching methods. You may find yourself in a lecture theatre with hundreds of other students so crammed together that you are sitting in the aisles, or in a smaller group in a relatively intimate atmosphere.

The lecture will normally last an hour, during which time the lecturer may present you with a clear, informative, well organised talk and presentation. On the other hand, it may be badly organised, lack substance and be extremely boring. Some lecturers welcome questions, others clearly do not, particularly when faced with large audiences and some complex or intense material to cover.

In the early weeks of the course you may find room clashes or missing lecturers may cause some disruptions to the planned timetable. At other times in the course lectures may be cancelled because of staff absence.

Seminars

The seminar is designed to enable discussion and interchange of ideas among its members. Ideally a seminar group is as small a group as possible (a dozen or so people) who take it in turns, under the direction of the lecturer in charge, to present a 'paper' to the other members of the group on an agreed question and topic. After a brief presentation of 10 to 20 minutes, the issues raised are open to discussion, clarification and debate in the group.

There are often problems with this format. The group may well be a great deal larger, which makes it difficult for everybody to contribute. Even smaller groups can feel intimidating whether you are presenting the paper or not. A common problem in seminars is a very few people dominating the discussion whilst a silent majority looks on. Lack of preparation, shyness and fear of ignorance being exposed, combine to keep many mouths closed.

Tutorials

A tutorial is an opportunity to look in some depth at particular topics or questions either in a small group or individually with a lecturer. Tutorial practices vary widely even within the same college. On one course you may have a *personal tutor* whom you can meet individually to discuss any concern you have in any area of your life as well as academically. This may be supplemented by a *small tutor group* in which the group can bring specific problems to be tackled by using both the expertise of the tutor and the group.

On a neighbouring course, there may be no personal tutorial system. In its place there may be something called a tutorial which may involve a large group (twenty or thirty people) many of whom get on with private study whilst a few seek the help of the lecturer. In such a group the lecturer may alternatively take the opportunity to pass on messages, give a mini-lecture on some problematic point or point out the error of some student's ways.

Any combination of these, and other, formats is possible in a tutorial system. It is well worth checking on the nature of the system on your course before you begin it.

Practical components

Workshops and *laboratories* form an important element of many courses not only in sciences and technology but also in the creative arts and social sciences. These are the times when by experiment and practical activity you attempt to link theory with practice and to advance your skill and expertise in design, investigation or production.

Field work can be a weekday activity in, for example, pursuing an on-the-spot investigation at a regular time during the week as part of your project work for the year. Field work can also involve special trips in Britain or abroad in term time weekends or weeks or even during the vacation. They can be among the highlights of a course year, incorporating visits to attractive locations with interesting practical investigations of a special topic.

Accommodation for these trips is usually basic but can involve a stay in a cheap hotel. These field trips can be invitations to excesses of all kinds so their success is often based upon the mutual respect that exists between the course staff in charge and students.

LEAs will reimburse money for some field courses if they are seen as an integral part of the course and necessary to its satisfactory completion. It is worth checking with both the course tutor and your LEA as to the chances of reimbursement.

Course work

The work undertaken week-by-week throughout the academic year both in college time and in your own time, is termed course work. This includes *writing essays* as well as preparing and presenting *seminars*. It can include writing up *laboratory or other reports* either informally or in a full, formal report form. For problem-solving, mathematically-based subjects it will include working through problems, tackling questions and worked examples.

Project work is another typical form of course work, particularly in the final year of many courses. *Reading* for a specific seminar or about an aspect of a particular topic is another common course work task. Many of these pieces of work will become vital parts of your year's assessment (*see* pp.73-74).

You may have a series of communication or general studies lectures to help you with some of these tasks, or study skills workshops, but not necessarily. Often you will be thrown back on to your own resources to cope with these demands. This is why developing your own ability to organise yourself becomes so important.

Using the library and resource areas

There's a story that one student who successfully completed a degree, visited the college library twice in a three year period: once to take a book out and the second time to return it. If it is true, it would be extremely unusual, for the vast majority of students use libraries and resources areas a great deal. In consequence, the heavy demand for studying space and for books and articles can cause problems in using them.

Yet it is well worth getting to know your library as early as possible during the course. It can seem overawing at first both in size and in the range of equipment being used. Most libraries provide several sources of help to overcome this problem.

Self-guidance booklets will guide you through the mysteries of the *microfiche* or *computerised cataloguing system*. Card indexes may still be around but are usually supplemented or replaced by the former systems. Many libraries run *induction courses* in the early weeks either as part of your course or as a separate venture. *Library staff* may be allocated to your area of study specifically to help you locate materials. *Study skills courses* may be organised by the library to help you read, take notes, find information, and so on, more effectively.

Computers and other resources

A large number of courses now involve some use of computing and there has been a large expansion of the range and availability of computers in colleges. As with the library, *beginners'* and more *advanced courses* are often organised and terminals can be booked for use for your own project or other work. *Self-guidance materials* are also produced by many colleges and *specialist staff* may well be available to help you.

Resources areas make available a wide range of facilities including photocopying, video and audio-taping, photographic and graphic services. Equipment and other services may be available for short loan either free or for a small charge.

GETTING DOWN TO STUDY

It can feel quite overwhelming when you are faced with so much private study time and a mounting pile of tasks to complete. It can be very hard to get down to work when faced with social temptations, some of which may invade your own room, such as visiting friends in a party mood.

One approach to help you get down to study is to find out how to set about taking notes, writing essays, reading and other aspects of studying in an efficient way. There are several useful books on the market to help you do so, several of which are included in the section on **Useful Reading** at the back of the book. In addition, a student counsellor, tutor or study skills group might help you find a sense of direction and motivation.

"The differential coefficient of... the differential coefficient of... the differen..."

Successful ideas

You will be helped to get down to study if you have some successful ideas you've already used in the sixth form or FE college. There is no one correct way to study. There are simply lots of good ideas that have worked for many students. You may find some of those ideas in the following series of suggestions for planning and organising study and improving concentration. Certainly, if you can master the skills of *questioning, summarising, time-allocating* and *task-setting* you are likely to be a very successful student.

Questioning

Try to use an active questioning approach in everything you do. Kipling's 'Why? Why? What? When? Where? How?' are useful questions in any study situation. When reading a book you can use them to turn headings into questions. For example, this section headed 'Questioning' can give rise to questions such as, 'What does he mean by Questioning?', 'When should I use questioning techniques?', 'How can I use it to read a book?'.

It is equally important to ask yourself questions about what you are
doing and how you are proceeding. For example, 'What am I reading this
page for?', 'Am I concentrating?', 'Do I understand it?' would all be useful
questions to be asking right now.

Summarising

The ability to pick out the most important — or *key* — words, data and con-
cepts from the vast amount of material you are presented with is going
to be another factor in your success. We all have to summarise, précis,
in everyday life. The temptation is often to use too many words in case
you miss out something important. This applies, for example, to reading
or taking notes from lectures.

You can try to develop your own skill at this by practising using fewer
words to catch the meaning of the passage. Many of these words will be
nouns, verbs or colourful adjectives.

One exercise would be to read a paragraph in a textbook and, as you
do so, ask yourself two questions:

1. What four words or phrases would I choose as the *main* words to
    summarise the contents of the paragraph?
2. What four words or phrases would I choose as those of secondary
    importance in the paragraph?

You could try this exercise with a friend and compare notes. Exactly
the same principal may be used to record key information from lectures.

Time-allocating

It's a good idea to get an overview of your use of time. A *chart* above
your desk can help if it shows your week's *timetable* and when your main
opportunities to work occur. Keeping a diary for one week, in which you
record exactly what you did and when, can give you a precise idea of how
the time has been spent. It can also pinpoint your *best time(s) of day to
study*. We vary in the times of day when we work best. You'll get down
to work more easily at the times that suit you best.

Finally, don't ignore *short periods of time* for routine study. An hour
between lectures can be filled with *both* a cup of coffee with friends *and*
10, 15 or 20 minutes spent on simple tasks such as finding a book, copy-
ing up some notes and jotting down a few thoughts for a seminar.

Task-setting

It's particularly important to see the *whole picture* of the task or tasks
that lie ahead of you, so that you can see how the small task you are tackling fits into the whole. Many students hesitate to do this as they fear they'll
panic themselves with the sheer volume of what they have to do. This may

happen momentarily when you've first listed, for example, what you have to revise for a subject. You can reduce this feeling to manageable proportions by using some *simple system of priorities.* You can use a simple symbol system to indicate what you know or understand of the topic, how easy or difficult you find it, how interesting it is to you and how useful it is. These four factors will help you decide what to do first other than simply relying upon urgency as a criterion for choice.

Incentives to complete tasks

So, for example, if you use some simple star (**) system, those topics which received the highest ratings would be the most tempting to revise first. As you would be most likely to be successful with these topics you will, as a result, boost your confidence and motivation.

Finding the natural breaks in topics will enable you to *tackle the whole task in parts,* nibbling away at it until the whole is completed. You'll encourage yourself to get these tasks done by giving yourself small *rewards* along the way, for example a favourite TV programme, a cup of coffee or a phone call to the girl friend or a pint down the pub when you've reached your target.

Such rewards can also help you improve your concentration.

"Read that lot! Now I'm off for a beer."

Improving concentration

Improving concentration is frequently either a matter of using more effective study approaches or resolving a personal concern which is interfering with your study. In the latter case, talking to someone may help, eg a friend, a relative, a teacher, doctor or counsellor, as described in Chapter 13.

Some of the following study approaches will aid your concentration.

1. Find a place to work which has a good feel to it. It should be a place that has enough light, heat and space around for books and papers. It should be a place you like to be.

2. Have all materials you need assembled around you from the start. Don't give yourself an excuse to postpone starting.

3. Devise questions to which you seek answers.

4. Be active in what you do, eg speak aloud, tape-record, talk to someone, write notes.

5. Pick topics to study which you already understand, find most easy to tackle and are of most interest or use to you, as well as those which are particularly useful or urgent.

6. Set yourself realistic small targets. This will give you more chance to succeed in reaching your goal. Success will both increase your self confidence and your work rate.

7. Vary both the topics you study and the methods you use.

8. Study for short periods of time, at least initially. 15, 20, 25 and 30 minutes can be very effectively used on routine study. Short breaks can be used constructively either for relaxation or recalling what you have been doing and planning what you're going to do next.

9. Rest and relax. Be positive about your breaks from study. Give yourself a day off a week at least and other free time when you are not obliged to feel guilty. A drink or a favourite TV programme can be used as a reward for the completion of a specific task. Physical exercise, such as a walk, a run, a swim, yoga exercises or team games, can help revitalise you, as much studying is relatively passive.

10. Check your sleep. Lack of concentration is often due to failing to look after a basic need for sleep.

HOW YOU ARE ASSESSED

One of the big differences between many higher education courses and an 'A' level course is the much greater importance placed upon course work in your final assessment. *Course work (see* p.67), together with your sessional (year end) exam results, will frequently be taken into account by the examination board which meets after marking is completed.

Some courses require that pieces of course work be completed by specific deadlines. Where the deadline passes, some penalty system may come into operation. Marks may be automatically reduced or lost altogether.

Other courses require that you pass tests on each stage of the course throughout the year, before being allowed to continue. This form of *continuous assessment* can be very rigorous. Some like it very much as they know where they stand all the time; others find it more stressful than conventional exams.

It is essential that you find out how your course will be assessed as part of your process of choosing.

Exams

Apart from conventional end-of-year exams which occur in May or June, there are other tests and mini-exams which may occur at other times on certain courses. Mid-sessional exams (halfway through the year) may either be simply a guide to your progress or be as important as the main exams themselves. Some individual lecturers may set objective tests of your knowledge in certain subjects, eg engineering. Exams before Easter are a common practice on some courses where students go off for a summer term placement.

The majority of students take their exams in May or June. Many exams are still of the conventional type — typically a 2½ or 3 hour paper from which some or all questions must be attempted in essay or problem-solving form.

Other forms of exam

You may also come across other forms of exam. Apart from exams with an *oral* (in higher education an oral is referred to as a viva), you may have a *practical* element in the exam. Other exams involve you seeing the questions beforehand so you are able to research the questions. Others may allow you to take books into the exam room. They may sound easy but they represent a testing form of examination and a clear examination of your study and intellectual skills.

You may find that your course has some specific form of examination not mentioned here. Check very carefully any information you receive about examinations so you know exactly what you are to face.

Coping with exam anxiety
Anxiety about examinations is common and if managed and channelled in the right way can also be helpful to exam performance. It is when the anxiety gets in the way that problems occur — panic, lack of concentration, inability to recall and physical symptoms can all result.

There are very clear ways of coping with exam anxiety and it is well worth your while seeking help if you experience it. Help will come in several forms. A *student counsellor* would be a very useful resource to help you find the source of your anxiety and to help you find ways of coping. A visit to the *doctor* may also help, particularly if you feel some medication might help you cope. You may also be able to talk to him or her about your concerns.

Groups and books can help
Some colleges, such as Plymouth Polytechnic, run *groups* on how to revise, take exams, cope with anxiety and relax. Learning specific ideas of how to revise and to organise yourself in the exam room can be a great help in coping with anxiety, as can specific techniques for relaxing and coping with anxiety. Sharing experiences with *other students* in the same position as yourself can be very helpful, particularly when you realise it's not only you who feels like this! You can also share good ideas, help each other with revising and lend encouragement.

Pitfalls
Here are some of the more common pitfalls students find when studying. Take care you don't fall into them!

— Finding yourself gazing for long periods of time at piles of open books or files with nothing much going on in your brain may be the commonest — inactive — study problem.

— Failing to develop a questioning, discriminating approach to your work and simply continuing to regurgitate the contents of a book or a page of notes.

— Becoming immobilised by anxiety about getting things done and then failing to cope with the anxiety.

— Misusing time — in particular, by an all-or-nothing approach which may involve a whole week or more doing no study of any kind and another week of doing nothing else but study.

10
Getting on with people

Going to college will certainly involve you in new relationships with parents, friends and your local community. Whether at home or away, you'll be establishing your own independent lifestyle, meeting new people, and entering new relationships. The new friends, the local people, the college staff and others you meet are likely to influence your relationships with those familiar people back home. Relationships may become strained as new pressures appear and this chapter is designed to alert you to some of these situations.

GETTING TO KNOW YOURSELF

The college experience can help you develop a clearer sense of who you are. And you are likely to know your likes, dislikes, beliefs and prejudices rather better as a result of the experience. Although many students feel they knew all about themselves well before going to college, the new people and situations often stretch and test that understanding. Often, without realising it, you've been cushioned from the reality of how friendships are made and conversations conducted by the familiarity of relationships back home.

The fresh start can be exhilarating. The freedom to try new lifestyles, new tastes or new images for yourself is made possible by a wide range of people and situations now available to you.

The fresh start can also be disturbing. Living independently can feel strange, facing you with uncertainties, homesickness or loneliness. It can leave you wondering about yourself.

Parents
'It was like losing an arm and a leg', was one parent's comment on her son's absence from home in the first term. Even if you're living away from home, parents are likely to continue to play a large part in your life. Your absence may cause a profound sense of loss at home.

Your feelings for your parents are likely to affect the pattern of weekly college life. Letters and phone calls take on significance in the week. The regular contact can be both a neccessity and a bind. The necessary struggle for independence can be as hard for you as their necessary 'letting go' can be difficult for them. As most students will still be dependent upon their parents for cash it is difficult to feel a full sense of independence, even if they want to do so.

You and your parents at home
If you are living at home, the relationship with your family is likely to change. You may be coming home at different times, perhaps late at night, or missing meals or staying out at night. Your sleeping, eating and studying routine may well be different from that of the past. New friends may well appear. All of these changes can involve some difficulties for you all and may cause clashes and arguments.

The hope is that over the period of college life you and your parents will come to realise more fully what is valuable in your relationships with each other. Some parents never feel able to let go of their children when they go to college and some students are unable to accept the responsibility of adult behaviour, staying in a childlike dependence, whether their parents want them to do so or not. At best, you will come to know each other as adults with respect and understanding of each other as people in addition to the love that already exists.

The girl or boyfriend back home
Going to college places many boyfriend/girlfriend relationships under considerable strain and many don't survive it. An awareness of this fact is often there at the time when decisions are being made about which college to go to and where. It can cause fears, possessiveness, upsets and rows or bring you and your special friend very close together.

It is quite possible to sustain and deepen your relationship whilst separated by distance and time. Weekends and vacations spent together can be marvellous times in the college year. Letters and phone calls can enable you to share your own different worlds and give your relationship continuity.

The college staff
The college staff do form a part of your everyday relationships. Many will only be seen in tutorials, lecture rooms, seminars, workshops or laboratories. Some you will also meet in specialist societies based upon the subject you are studying or in a sports club such as rugby. Although you'll find that relationships are likely to be more informal and more adult than your previous experiences, they will vary with the people you'll meet.

A guide to college staff appears in Chapter 2 (*see* pp.16-17) and to other helping staff in Chapter 13 (*see* p.95).

The local people

You may find you have a limited opportunity to meet local people if you're resident in a campus college. Apart from the cleaners, porters, janitors, canteen, shop or bar staff, you may find yourself cut off from ordinary life in the area. On the other hand, staying in lodgings with a family can involve you closely with local people, as can living in a house or flat in the town.

Getting to know the area and the people who live there is one of the great pleasures of going away to college. It's relatively easy to find yourself isolated from the area — apart from venturing into pubs — if you are campus-based and well worth making the effort to get to know the place and the people.

So what do students talk about?

As you'd expect, students talk about anything and everything, but there are certain recurrent themes.

Conversations will vary to some extent with the setting in which they are taking place. There are likely to be differences between conversations in the street, at a disco, in the Union or pub, in a club or society, at home or during a meal with friends.

'Shop' talk

Lectures or lecturers or work you have, or more likely haven't done. (This 'shop' talk is typical of many other groups besides students and can be a real bore and quite anxiety-provoking.)

Accommodation

Another common subject. Its distance from college, the people you live with, the damp patch in your room, the cost of it, the noise in it, etc.

Money

The late arrival of your grant, the early spending of it, or whether you can afford to go somewhere are typical themes.

The SU

What's happening there in the way of events and entertainment, the inadequacy of the facilities, or the Union executive and its politics.

Other people

Who you've met, what's happening to other people, who's doing what to whom, etc.

Booze and pubs
The best beer, cheap booze, the pubs with the widest range of real ales, the best pubs in town or in the country are all typical topics. Your drinking habits and the fresh excesses reached last night are others. This can become a real bore.

Parents and home
News from home or lack of it, troubles and difficulties in relationships with parents and your emotional ties.

The weather
Commentary and complaint about the 'bloody weather', whatever it's like.

The town or campus
Commentary and complaint about the town or campus, the fact that there's nothing to do, it's a dump, and so on.

Vacations
Enquiries about how vacations are going to be spent. How long will you be away? When will you be back? Are you going abroad this summer? etc.

Your health
The terrible cold you're nursing, the sports injury you've received, how you banged your ankle when drunk last night.

Transport and travel
How you are going to get somewhere, who can give you a lift, how much does it cost and how long will it take?

SMALL TALK

'Small talk' is a term used to describe many of the everyday topics of conversation exchanged upon first meeting and in other short meetings during the week. It is the type of conversation that occurs when you bump into someone from your course around the campus or in the street.

There will probably be times when you are stuck for something to say. Most of us have experienced a degree of awkwardness, even shyness, at some time or another. For some this feeling may be acute; for others, just a passing moment. Small talk can help fill the gap.

Conversations that are entirely made up of small talk would feel banal and shallow. On the other hand, the anxieties in first meetings and greetings are often real and it can help both to have an idea of what students talk about and how they do so. Additionally, some of the topics of small talk can also become significant and useful conversation — 'big' talk.

Guidelines to 'meaningful dialogue'

Asking questions
Finding out about what's happening or checking course assignments or being genuinely interested in someone else and their life.

Talking about yourself
We all have a need to talk about ourselves but you'll need to be certain that those around want to listen or people will start to hide when you appear. Not everybody wants to hear, for the fourth time, details of your canoeing expedition around the Serpentine.

"Can't really say I'm into small talk."

Commentary upon people, places and events
Discussions and analyses of what's happening, who's doing what to whom. This can be straightforward gossip, which can be both helpful and informative but one problem is that some people gossip maliciously.

Complaining
A common and eternal student theme. Students often feel like an oppressed minority and find many targets for complaint including the bank, the LEA, the government, the lecturers, the SU executive, the library, the weather, the beer, their accommodation, the social life. Basically, everything.

Humour
Spontaneous humour can be one of the great pleasures of life. A genuine course humourist is a popular figure. Stand up comedians are a different

matter and only the experts can sustain this form. Not everybody will be enthused at your laughing uproariously at your own jokes.

Sharing experiences and views
There's a need to share experiences and find out others' views, tastes and beliefs. One of the common early signs of this is the search in conversation for experiences you have in common with others or issues about which you can both agree. Another is suggesting meetings and activities to each other — a visit to the pub, a cup of coffee or an evening out.

Sharing anxieties
Using others to offload the things you're concerned about is an important part of relationships. Some guidelines are contained in Chapter 13.

Making friends

Nearly everyone hopes to make friends at college. It is a need almost everybody has in common, as is anxiety about making friends.

There is no magic formula. Some of the firmest and longest lasting friendships develop from the most unlikely combination of personalities and interests. Yet there are many features that will be present, to some degree or another, in all good friendships.

Good friends will be honest with each other and be there in times of upset or crisis. They will keep each other's confidences and be dependable. A sense of humour will frequently be shared, as may some interest or other. Sharing the same experiences can help sustain the friendship, but is not essential to it. In essence, a good friend is someone who just accepts you as you are.

Pitfalls
Here are some of the pitfalls many students find in trying to make friends.

● Seeing the girlfriend or boyfriend every weekend or going home very regularly can mean you've separated yourself off from the experience of college life. If the relationship breaks up, you can find it difficult to get in to college life and existing friendships.

● Choose your flat/house/room mates as carefully as possible as they are people you'll meet every day. First impressions can be very inaccurate when you've had only a short time to get to know people. Once you are living together, friends can feel very different as you battle with their used underwear, occupation of the bathroom or sour milk.

● The distress experienced by a friend can be almost as disruptive and disturbing to your life as it is to theirs. Try to avoid overloading yourself in your helping role — for guidelines *see* Chapter 13.

11
A full social life

A huge choice

One of the great experiences of going to college is the range of social life and recreation available to you. It is unlikely that you'll ever have been offered as much choice before in your life, or had as much time to do the things you enjoy. There is time to discover new activities such as tiddly-winks or hang-gliding. There is time to meet many different people in social and recreational situations such as clubs and societies. You'll have the opportunity to let your hair down or become an expert on real ale or dress as you want and develop your own way of life.

It also provides you with an opportunity to make a mess of things, by doing no work for weeks, for example. With luck (and some support) you'll untangle the mess.

This chapter focuses upon what's available in your Students Union (SU) and in your local area, recreational pursuits and the use of drugs.

STUDENTS UNIONS

SUs are big business. They generate turnovers of hundreds of thousands of pounds a year through their trading activities. They are run by elected officers drawn from the student body, supported by a group of paid employees. In larger colleges, many of these students will become sabbatical officers, that is, they will have a year off from studying in order to do the job and be paid a small salary to do so.

For a substantial minority of students, SU politics and intrigue become a major social preoccupation. Standing for election, canvassing, talking at meetings and taking part in hustings where candidates for election present their case can become an absorbing activity. Many hours can be whittled away writing letters to, or articles for, the student newspaper, or helping with the production of it. As each section of Union activity often has a committee to implement policy there is plenty of scope for direct involvement in power games!

Students Union events

Apart from the Freshers Week and beginning of term events described in Chapter 2, the Students Union via its various elected reps and committees organises many other events during the year. High on the list is entertainment. This involves bringing in bands and solo performers, theatre or dance groups and organising balls, discos and special event nights in the Union. Most SUs organise gigs by at least one or two of the current big name bands during an academic year and any other specialist local or less well-known ones.

As a result of all this activity, combined as it is with clubs, societies and the sporting and recreational facilities, SUs are usually very busy and well used by a high proportion of the student population. More so, where the social life in the local town is limited. The drawback of this heavy use is overcrowded and over-extended facilities and events.

Rag Week

Rag Weeks usually occur in the spring term. They are a week or so of exuberance in aid of charity in which, each year, students strive to outdo the ideas of past Rag Weeks in their attempts to raise cash. It is an excuse to be uninhibited, drink a lot and generally be very silly.

But it also brings students directly into contact with local people through collections, newspaper publicity (not always favourable), sales of (usually tasteless and tactless!) Rag mags, and radio and TV coverage of events.

The events of rag week are numerous. They will probably include discos, visiting bands, balls and other 'special' attractions. They'll also include sponsored events to raise cash — often feats of endurance of one kind or another, eg being pushed in a bathtub for 200 miles. Almost every conceivable idea has been tried at some time by students in Rag Week. For participants the sense of freedom and exhilaration are the important elements and this can lead to some conflict with the local community, particularly where excessive quantities of alcohol are consumed in such events as 'Drinking the Pub Dry'.

CLUBS AND SOCIETIES

Opinions vary as to how useful clubs and societies are in the social life of a college. They do provide an opportunity to meet students from other courses and, sometimes, other staff. They do give you a chance to try something new or to pursue a favourite hobby, hobbyhorse or leisure activity. Yet, unless you can attend regularly and meet a friendly group of people, you may find the experience rather barren.

How do you rate the clubs and societies?
You can use the checklist below to evaluate your Union clubs. A star system can show you its strengths.

*** Very good range
 ** Average range
  * Poor range

Then circle the particular activities that are important to you.

CHECKLIST: RATE THE CLUBS AND SOCIETIES

1. Sports Clubs
Range of activities and scope for participation? ☐

2. Subject Clubs
Societies or clubs in Geology, Psychology, Engineering offering events and social activities? ☐

3. Hobby Clubs
Chances to follow up your favourite obsessions like Chess, Dungeons and Dragons, Real Ale? ☐

4. Political Parties and Societies
A branch of the political grouping you'd want to join? ☐

5. Media
Chances to write on a mag or newspaper, collate or edit, review film and music, make videos? ☐

6. Religious groups
Your own faith represented by active groups? ☐

7. Cultural groups
Your own language and cultural group organising events? ☐

8. Drama and Art groups
Chances to participate and/or publicly perform in drama, dance, music, etc.? ☐

9. Voluntary Work Opportunities
Opportunities to become a Nightline volunteer, provide hospitality at Christmas, clean out a canal? ☐

10. Union Work
Involve yourself on a Committee in an official capacity? ☐

Rating union facilities

Several thousand students can troop through a Union building during a day, particularly at peak times such as lunchtime. Many Unions show both the wear and tear of heavy use and some are totally inadequate for the needs of students, making it more difficult to survive at college. You can use the Checklist below, together with the *rating scale on the previous page* to rate your own Union's facilities.

CHECKLIST: HOW DO YOU RATE THE FACILITIES?

1. Adequacy of space
Enough space to move around, find and meet others? ☐

2. Bars
Adequacy of serving area, range and price of drinks, atmosphere? ☐

3. Food
Good cheap food and a range for all eg good chips, vegetarian, cultural variations? ☐

4. Lounge and seating areas
Number and quality of quieter, conversation areas? ☐

5. Shops and Banks
Convenient bank, groceries, newsagents? ☐

6. Bookshops
Is there a college bookshop and how well stocked is it? ☐

7. Entertainment
Does the college have a hall large enough for the big named bands; a theatre for travelling drama groups? ☐

8. Recreational facilities in building
Range of indoor games and machines? ☐

9. TV/Video lounges
Do you have to do battle to watch a favourite programme or video? ☐

10. SU offices
Are the offices (and their officers) accessible and helpful, including the travel office? ☐

Sporting facilities

It's not just the SU that provides support to sports clubs and recreational activities whilst you're at college. The college will have its own PE and recreational unit, providing sports facilities, training and fitness facilities. If you're interested they will provide opportunities for you to play and take part in representative sport. There will also be recreational facilities provided in local town(s) and opportunities provided by the natural environment for your favourite pursuits.

College	*Civic Amenities*
Any Olympic standard facility?	(Opportunities to watch or play)
Swimming pool?	Major sporting venue?
Running track?	Range of top class sports clubs?
Squash courts?	(County Cricket, national
Sports Hall(s)?	basketball, etc.)
Outdoor, floodlit, playing area?	First or Second division soccer?
(for tennis, 5-a-side soccer, etc)	Golf courses?
Tennis courts?	Leisure Centres?
Golf course?	Parks?
Playing fields?	Swimming pools?
Soccer, rugby, hockey, etc.	Boating/sailing areas?

What the natural environment has to offer you will depend on your interests. Surfers will have different needs from potholers or hang-gliders. How you survive at college, if you know you don't like brick or concrete jungles, will depend upon the use you make of the open countryside, the sea, lakes and rivers, moors, mountains, hills and caves — and which are most important to you.

For further information about sports contact:

British Polytechnics Sports Association (BPSA), Room B223, Birmingham Polytechnic, Perry Barr, Birmingham B42 2SU (021-356 0009)
British Colleges Sports Association (BCSA)
Universities Athletic Union (UAU)
British Universities Sports Federation (BUSF)
British Students Sports Federation (BSSF)

Details of BCSA, UAU, BUSF and BSSF from
The Secretary (appropriate association), 28 Woburn Square, London WC1H 0AD (01-580 3618)

The local area

There is a great deal that goes to make up the atmosphere of the local area. It's often a combination of local views, amenities, social and recreational facilities. In reality, it is the mix of the town market, the Cathedral, the hills overlooking the town, the new shopping arcade, the riverside walk and the great pub in the town centre that creates the feel of the area.

Local towns

Local towns or cities are used in many ways. Entertainment facilities vary but all have clubs, discos, cinemas and theatres. Discos in town tend to be used by student clubs as well as individual students.

Shopping is a major social activity, particularly for clothes, cosmetics and consumer goods like records, tapes, CDs and videos. Good quality shops in an attractive shopping centre can make a great deal of difference to social life even if, as a broke student, your shopping is confined to Sunday window-gazing.

The public facilities of a town can likewise be very important, eg the parks and riverside walks. Sports and leisure facilities in towns are also widely used by students, particularly swimming pools, squash courts, sports centres, golf courses and horse-riding, and libraries, museums, craft centres and art galleries provide some of the aesthetic pleasures of life.

CHECKLIST: HOW DO YOU RATE THE TOWN?

Use the rating scale on p.83:

Discos	_____	Shops	_____
Entertainment clubs	_____	Good walks	_____
Concert venues	_____	Exhibitions	_____
Theatre	_____	Museums	_____
Opera	_____	Art galleries	_____
Ballet	_____	Historic buildings	_____
Art/Drama/Music centres	_____	Churches	_____
Restaurants	_____	Civic Sports facilities	_____
Pubs	_____	Access to nature	_____
Take-aways	_____	Parking facilities	_____

DRINK, DRUGS AND OTHER VICES

Alcohol

Alcohol is the drug most commonly used by students. It is socially accepted as part of student life and can easily use up large sums of money — £5 a night will soon eat away a grant. SUs are usually the cheapest places to buy it, particularly at certain times when 'happy hours' of cheap drinks or special brewery promotions occur.

Getting drunk, however, can become a way of life and a bore to you and others. It can become the only outlet for social life with rivalry in excessive drinking one of the many 'games'. Many mornings of hangovers with you saying to yourself 'Never again' may be the outcome. So will missed study.

Alcohol lowers inhibitions and relieves tension in small or medium doses (up to three or four pint equivalents), but it also acts as a depressant. Other drugs may do the same, but are socially less acceptable and are usually illegal or available by prescription only from a doctor.

The non-legal drugs

You'll certainly come across the use of illegal drugs during your student life. They'll be used by people you know or at parties you attend or in the house you live in. There may well be social pressures upon you, from friends or acquaintances, to use some drug or other — you are very likely to be offered what is around.

Much drug use is self-regulated by students. That is, attempts are made to enjoy their effects or minimise their harmful effects by using them in groups. Although they will vary in their degree of physical and psychological dependence, they will nearly always be expensive (although some can actually rival alcohol in cheapness).

Problems with drink or drugs?

If you're going to use legal or illegal drugs you'd be advised to know what you are using — and what it's doing to you! If you have difficulties — and a good proportion of students become alcohol dependent and heavy users of other drugs each year — then make use of the helping services described in Chapter 13.

In addition, some areas have local drugs information and counselling services and most towns have a branch of Alcoholics Anonymous.

Playing the machines and gambling

Many students spend a fortune on electronic, pinball and fruit machines as SU profits clearly show, many using the profits from the rows of machines in the Union to subsidise other services. Hours can drift by in the electronic jungle.

Others find the lure of the local casino is part of the freedom of social life that can be very costly. Addiction to gambling when you have created a lot of opportunities to do it can also be a problem needing help — *see* also Chapter 13.

Further help

Contact local branches of Gamblers Anonymous, Alcoholics Anonymous or Narcotics Anonymous. You can obtain the contact number from phone books, Samaritans or CAB, who will also supply the details of your local Council on Alcoholism, a useful organisation.

12
Love and sex

Love tends to have a will of its own in our human affairs. The time at college is often a time for discovery of love, intimacy and sexuality. Moving in and out of intimate relationships and in and out of love can be a major preoccupation, as can failure to do so. The ups and downs of the important relationships are likely to affect profoundly both studying and other close relationships with friends, flat-mates and family. Rivalries, jealousies, arguments and hurt may have been familiar in school days but can be intensified at college in a residential block, a close course group or a campus environment.

SEX — FANTASY AND REALITY

'I never did get invited to one of *those* parties' (Ex-student)

For many, student life provides a first taste of 'freedom' from living with parents. It provides more opportunity for entering into relationships. Having both the time and place in which to meet privately can provide more opportunity for sexual relationships to develop. This, and an outside world that still believes student life to be an endless round of sex and drugs and rock and roll (which it very often isn't), can also place pressure on you to enter into sexual relationships, even if you are uncertain whether you want to do so.

Failure to reach this imagined level of excellence can cause its own problems too. Like the ex-student quoted above you may put it down to never getting invited to those parties. Experience will probably show that 'those' parties are often no more than the product of an overactive imagination, stoked by alcohol with a small touch of the fisherman's tale about them.

Despite the existence of the opportunity for much sexual freedom, the majority of students do not appear to be engaged in one long sexual romp. Although many students experience 'one night stands' and one or more initmate sexual relationships in their time at college, promiscuity appears to be relatively unusual.

The 'hothouse' atmosphere

One of the common problems in college life is the 'hothouse' atmosphere that can develop in close personal relationships. In addition to the fact that you will often be mixing with a very narrow age range close to your own, life in a residential block or campus means it is difficult to escape from particular relationships.

If a relationship ends unsatisfactorily you may still be passing by each other in the corridor or sitting in the lecture theatre together or seeing each other across the Union bar. If you have been living together one of you can usually move out, even if that is not easy. It can be even more difficult if you are both on the same course.

Mutual friends and acquaintances can also wittingly or unwittingly intensify the situation, as your relationships are likely to be quite public.

Living together

Living away from home it becomes much easier for a relationship to develop to the point where you both want to live together. It can happen quite quickly at the point when living together feels more natural and right for the two of you. Often it follows a period when one of you has been staying overnight in the other's accommodation.

The majority of students share a flat or house at some stage of their college life. A proportion of these find they want to move their girl or boyfriend in. This can cause problems in altering the state of relationships, the space available and the costs of running the place. Sometimes it's necessary to move into a place of your own, especially if you were originally sharing a room with another person.

Living together changes existing relationships. You become more of an 'us' and sometimes continuing your individual friendship patterns with a member of the opposite sex can be difficult.

"How will I ever find someone as lovely as you?"

Marrying whilst at college

A minority of students decide to marry during their college courses. You'll still be in the student world, so life may not seem a great deal different. The contrast will be more evident if one of you is a student and the other is not or when you both cease to be students. You'll often find that little grant help is available from the LEA, particularly if you were assessed as a dependant student. Despite this, many students who marry find that they have a more secure basis for further study, because of their relationship.

SEXUAL IDENTITY

The majority of people are predominantly heterosexual being mainly attracted to people of the opposite sex. The term homosexual means basically the love of other members of one's own sex and an erotic attraction to them. Many people experience homosexual feelings at some times in their lives, eg adolescence, although they may not recognise them as such. As we live in a society that doesn't necessarily understand or tolerate differences from the heterosexual norm, we tend to paint exaggerated pictures of anyone who deviates from that norm.

It is not uncommon for students to go through a stage of uncertainty about their interest in and ability to make relationships with the opposite sex. Talking these uncertainties and fears through with a counsellor can be a helpful stage in clarifying these feelings. In addition, in some colleges a sexual identity group can be found, part of a national network called 'ID', it provides a social meeting opportunity.

The gay community

Virtually every college has its gay community and links with other homosexuals, male and female, in the town nearby. Meeting places are passed on by word of mouth — the pubs, clubs and discos where those on the 'scene' can meet. Some students decide to 'come out' and make public their homosexuality, but the pressures on homosexuals are still felt very keenly — prejudice and violence against gays are far from unknown. Gay Switchboard, available for at least part of the week in most towns, is a telephone contact service for many isolated homosexuals, and newspapers like *Gay News* provide another channel of communication to the millions of gay people in Britain.

CONTRACEPTION AND VD

Contraception

Parenthood is not always the deliberate and consciously taken decision it should be. One survey, conducted before AIDS publicity in 1987, showed that 60 per cent of students did not use any form of contraception the first time they had sexual intercourse. In the circumstances it is not surprising that there are unwanted pregnancies every year among students, despite easily obtainable contraceptive help.

There is no completely safe, harmless and easy to use method of contraception. However, there are a number of methods with very high reliability which make the prospect of an unwanted pregnancy extremely remote. The pill continues to be the most common form of contraception for females and the sheath for men. Chapter 13 gives more information as to how and where contraceptive help may be obtained and what to do if you become pregnant.

VD: Sexually transmitted diseases (STD)

VD means venereal disease, that is, any disease that is passed on by sexual contact. Only the three most serious are defined in law as venereal disease: syphilis (relatively rare), gonorrhoea and chancroid. Other STDs include herpes, genital warts, scabies, pubic lice ('crabs'), moniliasis ('thrush') and trichomoniasis ('trich'), and non-specific urethritis (NSU). They are passed on through sexual contact, although not necessarily sexual intercourse. It is not a proven fact that they are always sexually transmitted but generally sexual contact starts off or aggravates certain conditions.

If you engage in any sexual activity with another person you run some risk of catching an STD. If you are inattentive to personal hygiene, indiscriminate in your choice of sexual partners or promiscuous, you are likely to increase substantially the risk. Help is easily and confidentially obtained.

The AIDS issue

There's an inescapable reality about the AIDS threat to lives, and undoubtedly students are a potentially high risk group. The high risk comes both with freedom from home constraints and because many students are in a sexually active age group. It can also come with access to drugs that can be intravenously injected, with shared needle use producing a profound risk.

Alongside the fear of AIDS and of picking up the HIV virus from which it may develop, you may feel anger and frustration at the influence the AIDS issue is having on your own — and others' — sexual activity. You may be choosing to avoid intimate sexual contact altogether — or not to actively seek it.

The campaign for safer sex from 1987 onwards has resulted in a move away from 'wet' sex to the use of condoms in heterosexual and male homosexual relationships. It has also prompted some SUs and student health services to make condoms more easily and cheaply available. It is worth checking with your SU welfare staff, nursing or medical team to know the position in your college.

You can be at risk of contracting the virus through a variety of sexual behaviours, even if you're not being promiscuous. If you are in doubt about the facts of AIDS as they affect you, then call in to see a nurse, doctor or counsellor to talk over the issue or phone the Terence Higgins Trust (Helpline 01-242 1010).

13
When you need help

Help is at hand
This chapter looks at who you can turn to for help whilst at college and gives some guidelines on what you can do to help or be helped. It also gives guidelines for what to do if you face particular problems. You'll find tips on what to do about discontinuing, failing exams, exam anxiety, personal and sexual problems, money or legal problems, crisis of faith and coping with overwhelming feelings.

Who can you use as a helper?
This Checklist can be used as a guide should you need help in your life at college.

CHECKLIST: WHO CAN HELP ME?			
	Tick as appropriate		Tick as appropriate
Someone where I live	☐	Head of department	☐
Neighbour	☐	Lecturer/tutor	☐
Friend(s)	☐	Accommodation officer	☐
Relative	☐	Welfare staff	☐
Someone I know who has had the same problems	☐	The Students Union/NUS	☐
Student counsellor	☐	Nightline service	☐
Careers staff	☐	Citizens' Advice Bureau	☐
Chaplain	☐	Claimants Union	☐
Doctor	☐	Samaritans	☐
Nursing staff	☐	Others	☐
Wardens	☐	....	☐

HELPING AND BEING HELPED

There may be times when you feel the need for help, even if you consider yourself to be self-reliant and don't easily talk to someone else about a concern. You may be unclear about what is bothering you or uncertain as to what to do about it (so talk to someone). You may feel it is not worth bothering someone else with your problem (it is) or may feel it's a sign of failure to turn to another for help (it isn't). Even the most competent, confident and extrovert 'superstudents' may find themselves in these situations. Fortunately, for most students, competent professional help is at hand to support any help offered by friends, relatives and other agencies.

GUIDELINES FOR HELPERS

The essence of effective helping lies in respecting the other person and believing that, sooner or later, they will cope with their concern themselves. Helpers do not have to solve problems to be helpful, and do not have to give advice or tell people what to do.

At the heart of effective helping is attentive, active listening, for unless you are paying full attention to what the other is saying, you cannot be sure you have understood their concern. Your help is likely to be welcomed if it is not forced upon another and if you don't compare, judge or moralise about the other's situation. Simply accepting what is said and keeping it in confidence (a vital principle) can be an enormous help in itself. It is more likely to enable a person to express exactly how they feel, think or behave.

HELPFUL AND UNHELPFUL THINGS FOR HELPERS TO SAY

In negotiating help, certain things you say are likely to be more helpful than others. The examples below are followed by some comments on what makes them helpful or unhelpful.

Examples of helpful questions or statements

'Do you want to talk about it?'
'Is there anything I can do to help?'
'Let me know if I can help in any way'
'Do you want any help with anything?'
'How are you feeling?'

These questions or statements tend towards 'openness' in the sense that they give alternatives and don't restrict the replies. They offer help without forcing it and they accept feelings.

Examples of unhelpful questions or statements

'It's not worth worrying about'
'Cheer up'
'Pull yourself together'
'Get a grip on yourself'
'Don't worry'
'Everything will be all right'
'Your brother/sister/cousin Geoffrey, never had this problem'

"It's high time these went back to the library!"

These statements tend to be anxiety-laden and are often used repetitively. They tend not to accept feelings. They tend towards nagging and they offer uninvited advice. In addition, they tend to be too generalised and may even compare you, adversely, with another person.

WHO ARE THE HELPERS?

In addition to any friends or relatives and the tutors and lecturing staff
mentioned in Chapter 2, there are others who play a part in the college
helping services, some of whom do so on a full-time basis.

The Head of Department

A good head will ensure that staff work well together in the interest of
students as well as themselves. You can approach a good head over issues
like problems you have at home, failure in some assignment or even
whether to drop out. The less useful head will be more preoccupied with
the paper on his desk and hassles with his colleagues. He may give you
lots of advice in a very short interview if, of course, he's got the time.

The Academic Registrar

The head of a most useful and important team in college, the academic
registrar is concerned with the efficient administration and conduct of
much student business, like admissions and grants. They can be approachable and student-orientated.

The Finance Officer

You'd be most likely to meet the college finance office team if you have
money to pay or you are owed money by the college. They are concerned
with the vast budget of the whole college, but the best are able to keep
the interests of individuals in view. If you're unlucky enough to get one
of the others and you've failed to pay something it will feel like being
pursued by Ghengis Khan and his hordes of Mongol warriors.

The Accommodation Officer

The accommodation officer and his or her team are concerned to provide
a comprehensive service. Most will want to be approachable and efficient,
and see your welfare to be an important part of their role.

   Because of the difficulty of the job, in attempting to provide a service
for both students and landladies/landlords, accommodation officers are
often criticised.

The Careers Adviser

Careers advisory services in colleges are the firm link with the world of
work. Many are good and offer a very comprehensive service. Careers
advisers will offer individual interviews if you are unsure of your course
or career or require information, and the office maintains a full and informative careers library. The worst deal you are likely to get is an
overstretched service with long queues for information or interview.

Welfare staff

Welfare staff may be employed by the college or the Students Union. They may be called welfare officers or go under other titles such as student services officers. Sometimes the role is coupled with that of the accommodation officer.

Welfare staff will be a source of information, guidance and practical help on matters like grants, money problems, housing benefit, visa problems, disputes and legal difficulties.

"Hello, is that student services? Hello? Hello?"

Students Union

The SU has elected executive officers who may well offer help and assistance with your concerns. They may take up your case in the event of some academic problem, such as an appeal against an exam board decision, or may make representations to the college authorities on behalf of a group of students in difficulty. At best, you'll get conscientious and thorough help with national back up from NUS and other agencies. From less experienced or conscientious executive officers you may get less real help.

Nightline service

There are student-run overnight helping services in many colleges called Nightline services (the name may vary from one college to another). They aim to provide an information service to students coupled with a listening and befriending service. If you are lonely or troubled during the night they offer a phone-in or call-in service. If you call in you'll usually be met by one or two students, offered a cup of tea and made to feel at home.

Many services emphasise that they are not just a crisis service but a service for all students. Many offer other services, for instance message passing services.

Nightline is run by volunteer students. They will usually have a stall at Freshers Fair-type events. Becoming a Nightliner can be a rewarding experience, even if the service isn't heavily used (although some are). You'll meet students from other courses and come to know them well through a training programme, usually run by counsellors or psychologists as well as experienced Nightliners. You will also find out more about yourself and gain help for yourself by being on duty with others.

Doctors

It is advisable to register with a doctor when studying away from home and you'll need to take your medical card with you when you register. Some colleges provide their own medical service, so it may well prove convenient to register with the college service whose doctor(s) will be attuned to student problems. However, check that the surgery hours enable you to visit the doctor easily without disrupting your course timetable.

If you are seriously concerned about your own mental health and find yourself wondering 'Am I going mad?', 'Am I heading for a breakdown?', talk to a doctor or counsellor about your concern. Doctors may refer you to a student counsellor if they see this as appropriate. They also have links, as do many counsellors, with psychiatric help for those who feel in need of it.

Nursing services

Most colleges have an experienced nursing officer who is available for a wide range of concerns. A nurse is often a first port-of-call for you when you are anxious about some aspect of your physical well-being. Apart from first aid, injections and general advice and guidance on health matters, the nurse may offer a limited dispensing service, such as for female contraceptives, and continuous back up treatment for a physical complaint. Many nurses may also be effective listeners, supplementing the work of their colleagues.

The chaplain

This may be one person or a team of people whose main concerns are the spiritual needs of all students and the quality of life of the college. As well as running the more formal theological activities such as services, prayer meetings and the like, they can also be found getting to grips with everyday life — running lunches, student evenings or even chatting over a pint in the Union bar.

Earnest, pious, righteous, God-fearing, fire-and-brimstone types do exist and pop up from time to time to pontificate on the virtues — or otherwise — of their students. Luckier colleges find that their chaplain is a real asset to the spiritual and secular life of the place.

The student counsellor
The counsellor offers a confidential helping service, whatever concern you have. You will be accepted as an adult and given help and support to resolve problems for yourself. It is a reliable and useful service for all students. You may be reluctant to bring yourself to see a counsellor. On the other hand if you want to see one, you may have to wait a few days, as the service tends to be well used by students.

Careers information officers
Careers information officers are careers staff with responsibility for the provision of information on careers in universities and polytechnics. They act as support staff to careers advisers and are available for careers enquiries when you call in to the well-stocked careers information rooms for which they are responsible. They are very useful helpers providing a firm link between the college and the world outside, as well as other helpers such as careers advisers and counsellors.

Wardens
A warden acts as an overseer of life in a student hall of residence. They may live on site or close by, and have overall responsibility, usually with another member of the college staff, for the day-to-day running of the hall. It is a difficult task involving every role from befriending to policing.

Wardens are either paid a small sum for their work or are offered free or cheap accommodation in lieu. They are often younger staff or researchers who are prepared to take the responsibility and hassle that accompanies the role, and can be very useful in generating and maintaining good hall relationships. They may also be supported by certain selected 'senior' residents, older students acting as a support system for the newcomers.

Other helping agencies
Many students make use of the widely available national network of helping agencies. In particular, the Citizens' Advice Bureaux, the Samaritans and Family Planning Clinics are widely used by students as a result of their useful and effective services. Other specialist groups are also in demand, if less well known. Among these are the Claimants Union for claims on the DHSS, and Release which specialises in help for those with legal and other problems related to the use of illegal drugs.

SPECIFIC PROBLEMS

Thinking of leaving?
Many students have doubts about whether they've done the right thing in coming to their particular college. Many of those doubts surface in the

first term. It can be very difficult to believe that things will improve when things aren't going well. A large majority of them find that their doubts subside when some good things happen or when they get used to things which seemed strange in the early days and weeks.

Transferring to another college or course

However, if early on in your first term you discover that you have made the wrong choice, it may be possible for you to transfer elsewhere, in that Autumn Term. This is dependent on discovering your mistake early (in the first few days/two or three weeks). It is also dependent upon having the appropriate qualifications and aptitudes for another course and being accepted by them ie they both want you and have a place available.

What to do

Approach another course and ask about the possibility of transfer. They will ask for a supportive letter from your outgoing course, which, once received, will be followed by an acceptance. Inform your LEA and ask for the grant/fees to be transferred to the new course. This is usually a formality.

You can sometimes transfer from one course to another at the end of the acadamic year. You will almost certainly have to start a first year course again if the course/subject content differs from your on-going course. Where courses are compatible, you may be able to move from a first year course at one college to the second year course at another. Consult your college careers service and the ECCTIS (Educational Counselling and Credit Transfer Information Service) booklet in your careers information room.

Why discontinue — and when?

You are most likely to discontinue or 'drop out' in the first term of your first year, if you are going to do so. Other crises points frequently occur in the first week or two of the Spring Term and in the middle of the second year, when you can lose your sense of purpose.

The most common reasons for dropping out involve deciding you've made the wrong choice of course/subject/institution; finding you've no motivation of your own to do the course; difficulty in settling in to a less structured environment and personal problems. Personal problems may include missing friends, family, boy or girlfriends. They can also include problems with accommodation or not feeling happy in the town or geographical area in which the college is located.

Talk to experts

Talk to experts who can give you sound guidance of an objective kind, as well as your family and friends. You will normally find staff are helpful, even when you are planning to leave the course. Counsellors and careers advisers will provide you with objective help in your decsion-making. Welfare staff will be able to give you accurate information about grants and fees.

Guidelines on discontinuing

● As the grant regulations stand in 1987, you are entitled to a one-term mistake without it affecting your right to a mandatory award. This applies if you discontinue at the end of the first term, *not* if you return in the Spring Term.

● You do not have the automatic right to a grant for 3 or 4 years if you change course. A grant (for maintenance and fees) is payable for a specific course: change courses and the situation changes.

● Remember that even if you do not receive a maintenance award from an LEA, it is worth applying for a grant, as your fees will be paid. You'll have to find the cost of them yourself if you don't apply.

● You won't have to pay back maintenance grant which covers the weeks you have legitimately attended your course. If you leave before the end of the Autumn, Spring or Summer terms, you'll have to repay money paid to you for the weeks you haven't attended, plus any money paid in the grant for vacation payments.

● If you leave in the Spring or Summer terms consult beforehand, if possible, your LEA to find out their attitude towards any grant for future study. You'll normally forego your right to a mandatory grant for a future course.

● There are circumstances in which you may be entitled to a *mandatory* award for a second course immediately following your first year's course in higher education, if the first course has failed to meet your *educational need* (a key phrase). Check with your experts to see if the regulations apply to you.

Useful reading
Notes for Guidance for Discontinuing Students, AGCAS/CSU
Careers Information Booklet
NUS Welfare Manual

Exam anxiety

It is certainly possible to cope with exam anxiety. Counsellors can be a very useful source of help in enabling you to cope. Your college may run groups on revision and exam techniques. There may be groups for those feeling very anxious in which you can learn methods for coping or relaxation classes where you can learn a few simple and effective relaxation techniques. Other services, like the medical services, can be useful for some students as well.

Learning the techniques of revising for and taking exams can in themselves relieve exam nerves. Books can give some guidelines on these approaches, eg *How to Pass Exams Without Anxiety* Acres(1987) contains guidelines for how to cope with anxiety by the use of thinking, visualising, breathing and muscular relaxation techniques. Some colleges produce student guidance notes, often available in the library.

Failed exams?

It is well worth checking before you start a course what the failure rates are for it, particularly for the first year. For a good many years many courses, particularly in engineering, technology and some science subjects, have had high first year failure rates (as much as 25 or 30 per cent in some cases). Whether or not your own likelihood of failure is high, many students will fail one or more exams during their time at college. Examination regulations, which vary from course to course and college to college, will determine whether or not you are able to continue the course. Frequently, there are options to continue study. You may be able to transfer to a course at a lower level, eg degree to HND. On the other hand, you may be able to argue that the course does not meet your educational needs (*see* the section on *discontinuing*). Appeals, resits or retakes may be possible (*see* below). If none of these are possible, there are frequently clear employment opportunities for those who don't complete higher education. All is not lost, even if it feels that it is. Talk to a counsellor, tutor, head of department or careers adviser about your situation.

Appeals

There is a formal appeal structure for many courses. It lays down the conditions for an appeal and how to go about it. However, in many colleges, few appeals are successful, so it is well not to build up high hopes. Students Unions, welfare or counselling agencies may help you formulate your appeal.

Resits

Resits are really quite common in the early years of courses. Where one subject (perhaps at most two) has been failed, an opportunity is provided to resit the exam, usually before the start of the next term. Many students pass their resits and continue on the course thereafter.

If you fail a resit you will usually not be allowed to continue the course until you have satisfied the examiners that you are able to do so. Vacation periods can be ruined by the prospect of resits at the end of them. For other courses, you will not be allowed to continue with the course at all if you fail the resits.

Retaking the year

You may be offered the chance to retake a year. If you do so, you may have a choice of full or part-time attendance and, for a few courses, a choice of retaking the exams without attendance, if you have satisfied the course-work requirements. In general, LEAs will not fund you with grant or fees to retake but in exceptional circumstances, with support from your college and, perhaps, medical evidence, an additional year's grant may be awarded. Your counselling and welfare services can provide guidance on this issue.

Personal and sexual problems

Many students have problems with their personal life which arise directly from sex, love and relationships. Often these may be embarrassing and you may feel very sensitive about them. But chances are they will not just go away. In fact trying to put some problems out of your mind in the hope that they will just get better on their own can even be dangerous.

Help for VD sufferers

You can find descriptions of the symptoms of various venereal diseases in many books easily obtainable in bookshops. College Welfare and NUS Welfare handbooks also contain descriptions and guidelines and the Health Education offices issue free guidance notes.

If you have any doubts or worries it is important both for your own health and those you may have come into sexual contact with that you contact a doctor or go to a local special clinic. There is no need to feel embarrassed or ashamed and your visit will be kept as confidential and private as possible. It is very important to be honest with them so that contact tracing can occur to protect the health of another or the life of an unborn child (which may be affected by a number of STDs).

Special clinics and treatment

Treatment in special clinics is easy, the clinic staff are usually pleasant, can't be shocked and won't pass judgment on you. Anybody who is worried should go along. The treatment usually consists of antibiotics, ointments, lotions and pessaries, or may take the form of capsules or injections, according to the nature of the STD. You will be asked not to make love in the first few weeks of the treatment.

There are usually separate clinics for men and women. You may take a friend with you if you are feeling nervous, although they may be asked to wait in reception. You and your sexual partner may visit together if you wish.

Contraceptive help
Contraceptives and advice are available free of charge to men and women from Family Planning Clinics (addresses in the local telephone directory). The same confidential service is also offered by doctors and college health services, although doctors cannot prescribe sheaths free of charge. Both Family Planning Clinics and college health services expect and hope students will seek contraceptive advice and help, and obtaining it should be straightforward and easy. Problems with contraceptives can also be discussed with the nursing service which may exist in your college.

Other sexual problems
You may find unexpected problems in your relationships whilst at college. You may have problems in making or sustaining relationships. Fear, guilt or shame may be affecting some aspect of your sexual relationships or preventing you from forming intimate relationships. Shyness, self-consciousness and anxiety are other concerns which may cause problems.

The counselling and medical services are two clear sources of help. The local Marriage Guidance Council may well be able to help point you in the right direction too. Certain bodies exist to help with specific difficulties, eg the Albany Trust to help homosexuals and other individuals with other difficulties.

Pregnant
If you want to discover whether or not you are pregnant, many college medical services will send away a specimen of urine for analysis as a confidential service. You can also carry out your own pregnancy test for about ten pounds. Your chemist is one source of information; national agencies are others.

If you decide you want to continue your studies through pregnancy until your child is born, you will find the majority of colleges are very helpful and accept your situation well. But whether it is feasible to continue will depend upon your good health and the timing of your examinations.

If your pregnancy is unwanted and you are considering termination, you will probably first discuss your decision with your doctor. A counsellor, nurse or welfare officer may also be helpful. Nationally, the Brook Advisory Centres and the British Pregnancy Advisory Service provide practical help and advice about abortions. The 'Life' service, widely advertised, will provide encouragement and support should you decide *not* to terminate a pregnancy.

Money problems

Money problems are among the most difficult to resolve. There are sources of help available but many of them are limited in scope or availability. Although many money problems actually start with the bank, the first person to approach is the bank's student adviser or equivalent. Overdraft facilities are limited but the bank may well lend a sympathetic ear.

If this is unsuccessful there are certain educational charities that may be able to help. Details of these are contained in the publications listed in **Useful Reading** at the back of the book. Some colleges have a trust fund for loans, usually for smaller amounts over limited periods of time. The DHSS may be approached in some circumstances for crisis help.

You'll need further guidance on all of these — and other — options which is best provided by college welfare services or the Citizens' Advice Bureau.

In trouble with the law

Students fall into the age and income groups that are at risk of being in trouble with the law; they also tend to look like 'students'. Three of the commonest reasons for using legal services for criminal or civil law disputes are motor vehicles, landlords/landladies, and the use or abuse of alcohol or other drugs.

Useful agencies

The college may well have contacts with a free and confidential legal service, sometimes provided by law lecturers at the college. Many SUs have legal contacts, and the NUS offer guidelines on many issues. There is the additional help of Law Centres in many cities and in nearly every town the Citizens' Advice Bureau has a legal service that is easily approachable and well used.

Your own college SU, welfare or counselling service is likely to have contact names and addresses for local solicitors involved in the Legal Aid Scheme. This scheme offers very cheap, or even free, legal advice for low income groups. Release, based in London and one or two other cities, is helpful for guidance on illegal drug offences. Nationally, the National Council for Civil Liberties is a useful pressure group and source of guidance on the infringement of rights.

Crisis of faith

Spiritual, ethical and moral dilemmas may accompany your time in college. You may have a crisis in your existing faith or come upon a spiritual belief for the first time. You may discover other faiths and beliefs which appeal to you. Your studies may result in new perspectives and ideas about life. Indeed, the whole experience of college can feel overwhelming and fundamentally challenge you as a person.

Many groups and individuals can offer such spiritual help. The chaplaincy service is one; full or part-time chaplains of different denominations open to those of all faiths or none. Religiously based groups and societies in colleges provide another network for conversation and, hopefully, support.

Trouble at home

If trouble occurs at home, an illness or crisis of some kind, you may want to return home to add your support. Speak to your tutor or head of department to inform them of the situation and you will find a sympathetic approach. If you are in doubt about what to do or if the problem is a protracted one, then talk it over with someone like your personal tutor or a counsellor.

Accommodation problems

Just about every agency can be helpful in some way in regard to accommodation problems which are among the most common types of difficulty. Several of the helpers in the checklist on p.95 could be useful. In particular, the accommodation officer, SU, welfare or college welfare staff and wardens would offer help where relevant. Local Housing Advice Centres can be particularly useful, as can Citizens' Advice Bureaux. The DHSS can be approached for cash help, too.

Anxious, depressed or lonely

Each of these feelings is commonly experienced by students. Most of us feel anxious or depressed or lonely or some combination of the three at some stage in our lives. How intensely we feel them and for how long will vary. If you are concerned about your own feelings of anxiety or loneliness or depression lasting for days or weeks, talk to someone about it. Locate your resources from the checklist on p.95. Once again, a student counsellor is likely to be very helpful and your doctor may give you some helpful guidance and treatment.

Suicidal feelings

If you experience feelings of wanting to die, the chances are you're feeling very unhappy and desperate. You may be feeling there is no way out of the position in which you find yourself. You may be feeling very angry. However intense and real your feelings may be there are certainly threads of hope which others can help you find. Talk to a friend and bring yourself to a competent helper — a counsellor would be of enormous help. The Samaritans and other telephone/call-in services exist for exactly the same purpose — to be there to befriend you in your time of need.

If it is a friend or acquaintance who is threatening suicide, take them seriously. Offer what help and listening you can and encourage them to use the services available.

Pitfalls
If you find yourself in the position of lending someone an ear or otherwise helping make sure you avoid the following pitfalls.

● When trying to help you can spend many hours lending an ear to some on-going problem. In doing so you can feel very over-stretched as a helper. You can feel overloaded or inadequate.

● One of the problems is that many of your friends feel stressed and vulnerable at exactly the same time as yourself, perhaps around exam time. In consequence you are not in the best frame of mind to help them (this is a dilemma of helping jobs generally).

● There are a few religious sects that make a special point of attracting new students to their organisations. They know the vulnerability of those away from home for the first time and you may find yourself being invited to do a free personality test or answer a questionnaire, both of which are designed to encourage you into expensive commercial organisations.

14
Special circumstances?

This chapter focusses upon the special circumstances of those who are part-time students, those who are single parents, disabled, mature students and those from overseas.

Part-time students

It can be very difficult to keep up a momentum to study when you are a part-time student. You may well feel more isolated than full-time students and feel a great deal of pressure on your own ability to organise yourself. You can continue to use college services in full, however, although your access to some lecturing staff may be limited. Use the full range of services to help with issues like cash and keeping your motivation to study — welfare and counselling would be particularly useful.

The DHSS place many obstacles in the way of drawing Supplementary Benefit whilst studying part-time, so don't assume you'll automatically be able to pursue your studies part-time when unemployed. You'll have to be on a genuine part-time course, which you are prepared to leave if you receive a job offer. You will also have to fulfil a number of other conditions.

Single parent

Being a student as a single parent is one of the tougher situations. Many single parents manage it remarkably well but not without the cost of a great deal of stress.

If you are on a course with other mature students or others in your situation you may well find self-help co-operation can be a big boost. Even with childless students around you, you may find support for occasional babysitting. Many single parents, however, rely heavily upon neighbours or other close family for support.

Where child-minding facilities do exist it is often difficult to afford them. Many colleges, however, have no effective support for single parents. A few do have creches, so it's well worth checking them out if you have the option to move geographically. Check carefully also, your grant entitlement and the DES Hardship Scheme. These may be of term-time help. In making some sense of the tangle of rules and regulations the college welfare services may be, again, just the job.

Disabled students

Hopefully you will have checked the support and resources available to you before you went to your college. However, promises may not have been kept, by omission or design, and resources which appeared adequate can turn out to be less so.

Disability ranges across a very wide range of limitation and the disabled are not one homogenous group. There are, however, some guidelines for surviving the system, particularly when circumstances feel stacked against you.

- Seek out other students with a similar disability to yourself and form yourself into a formal or informal alliance. The Academic Registry should be able to provide you with the names and course attended by others. Consider forming your own support group, eg a dyslexic students support group was formed at Plymouth Polytechnic.

- Approach the Students Union, library, welfare and counselling services as well as your own lecturers and state your needs, long and loud, if necessary.

- Draw attention to your situation by approaching a formal college committee concerned with disability as they should be an important pressure group.

- Alert your department and course tutor to any difficulty you are experiencing or any resource inadequacy. Support the notification with documentary evidence wherever possible, such as medical notes or the results of tests. Do this before crisis points like exams.

- Contact the National Bureau for Handicapped Students (NBHS), for guidance at NBHS, 336 Brixton Road, London SW9 7AA (01-274 0565).

Mature students

Relationships at college and home
It can feel very strange, and difficult, in the first term. Being surrounded by younger students can cause you to feel vulnerable. Adjusting to being without earnings is likely to be difficult if you were in work before. Some college staff can be difficult to relate to and may feel threatened by you. At worst, you'll find yourself patronised or disregarded and may lose something of your sense of self.

You are likely to find that your life experience helps you relate well to many of your younger contemporaries. Younger students may well beat a path to your door as an approachable older human being. It is in the disruption of everyday existing relationships — with family and friends — that difficulties most frequently occur as adjustments continue to be made to the daily, weekly and monthly routine, for instance children may well struggle to adapt to the new role their parent is fulfilling, with its different status and identity.

Intimate relationships
The image of the swinging sixties is taking a long time to lie down and die, especially in relation to student life. Mature students may hold an image of college sex life that is millions of miles from the truth. Students in general have a good many problems with close relationships and sex, and for the single mature student this task is no easier. They have the additional problems of age differences to cope with.

For married students the problems are different but can be as complicated, especially if your spouse is not connected with the college. Problems of trust may occur as misunderstandings arise. The possibility of close relationships forming with fellow students can be a confusing and worrying experience for your partner. And the greater freedom at college may lead to fear of affairs and emotional entanglements.

Cash issues
You may find money issues are likely to be uppermost in your mind during the year. Although you should be receiving extra cash in your grant as a mature student, it's still likely to be difficult to make ends meet. Check with welfare agencies to see what other help is available, eg the DES Hardship Scheme. Where your course involves a placement, eg social work, you may well find the level of expenses you are able to claim are totally inadequate. Some students say they've had to find up to £200 extra per annum to see them through. Even where expenses for travel are paid (which is rare) you may find delays occur in reimbursement.

Settling down to study
You will probably find that studying techniques are one of the aspects of college life that causes you most anxiety in the first weeks. Put some effort in the first few weeks into learning effective techniques that suit you. You can gain particular help by talking to others and sharing both difficulties and ideas that work. The college study skills programmes will be useful for you as will books like those mentioned in the section **Useful Reading.**

Booklists can feel overwhelming. Don't buy books until you are sure they will be useful. Don't blindly read books: booklists are designed to be used selectively and each book does not have to be read from cover to cover. Your concept of standards will take some time to form, inevitably. Take guidance on common 'faults', like the over-use of personal experience and the personal pronoun 'I' in social science essays, over-revising for exams and exam panic. Help should be at hand!

Help for mature students
Self-help with other mature students and within your own family can be of great value at this time, as can checking out the various helping services. Meeting other, particularly second year, mature students can be especially helpful — ask your tutor or the SU or counselling/welfare agencies if they can help in arranging something along these lines.

At the same time talk it over with someone, for your new lifestyle is likely to be causing pressures at home. You may feel you 'ought' to be old enough to stand on your own feet . . . don't let that prevent you using the excellent services that are normally available. You'll be helped to help yourself and, hopefully, feel more resourceful after the experience.

Useful Resources
The SU Welfare Office; The College Counselling Service; The College Study Skills Programme.

Useful Books
Acres, David (1987) *How to Pass Exams Without Anxiety,* Northcote House.
NUS Welfare Manual (annual).

Overseas students

Your first term
All non-commonwealth students (other than European Economic Community nationals) must register with the police within 7 days of arrival, and it costs £5 to do so at present.

You may find your college has some welcoming scheme for you — an overseas students meeting or social evening. The International Friendship League (IFL), which has branches throughout the country, may invite you to a social evening, and the YMCA or YWCA organisations may provide a welcome locally.

However, you may find other attitudes less welcoming and something of a shock. You may be used to open, welcoming, friendly attitudes and find they are not present in those you meet. You will probably be a very serious and hard working student and may find some home students seem uninterested in their studies. Your pride in being at college may contrast with other students' attitudes.

The Christmas vacation can be a particularly difficult period. You'll want to avoid loneliness so try to arrange to visit friends or take advantage of any hospitality offered by English families. Some welcoming schemes for overseas students are organised by Christian groups of the IFL or the college chaplaincy.

Practical issues

Money, accommodation, health and food are likely to be every bit as important to you as an overseas student as to your home student contemporaries. Problems can be caused from the outset by the difficulty of finding suitable *accommodation,* particularly if you are attempting to find self-catering accommodation close to college and bring your family.

Restrictions on the transfer of *money* is another common difficulty for students from some parts of the world — it can cause the most severe stress. You are not allowed recourse to public funds, such as housing benefit, when money fails to arrive. You may find the cost of living higher than you expected, for instance the cost of heating your accommodation in winter.

Most *medical* services are likely to be free or at low cost. Register with a doctor at an early stage; the doctor's receptionist will explain what you have to do. Ensure you choose a doctor close to your home or one that you can visit without it affecting your lectures.

Food may appear tasteless and lack variety in the early days until you track down ingredients to cook for yourself.

When taking *vacations* overseas ensure you have evidence for re-entry. Plan out your vacations so that they have variety, or otherwise they can feel very barren.

If restrictions apply to your passport you'll not be able to *work* legally. Vacation or part-time work could involve you in the risk of deportation.

Relationships and attitudes

The attitudes of the British towards overseas students vary a great deal according to your personality, ethnic group, colour, religion and lifestyle. Black or brown skinned students are likely to experience more racialist attitudes than white skinned overseas students. You may well find you miss your family and friends back home a great deal and feel lonely at times. There may be cultural gaps with other students; 'small talk' may not always be easy and your accent not always understood even if English is your native language. You'll probably find, however, that you will form good relationships with some other course members as well as others in the same situation or same culture as yourself, particularly as time goes on.

A lot of people frequently misunderstand sexual attitudes in the UK. The level of permissiveness is sometimes over-estimated, but just as often underestimated. But attitudes to love and sex can be as old fashioned as ever, and open approaches are not always welcomed.

Love at first sight is not unknown but more often than not it takes a good deal of time to develop. On top of this, attitudes to skin colour, race or religion can often interfere with relationships too.

It can be a lonely and sexually frustrating experience being a student in Britain, particularly if your partner is in your home country or if you meet few people who understand your cultural and social needs.

Studying

Many overseas students work very hard indeed. Some work too hard, seeing breaks from study as a subtraction from the working process. They are not; they are a part of good study techniques. Hard work alone is not enough and many overseas students fail to learn effective ways of studying, so the ideas in Chapter 9 may be particularly relevant. Teaching methods can feel strange as can the attitudes and expectations of lecturers towards your studying. If language is a problem, many colleges provide special English classes.

Problems? — Useful people and organisations

College counsellor; Students Union welfare staff; accommodation officer; your personal tutor; your doctor; local religious or cultural societies (many in the SU) eg Christian or Muslim groups, an African society or Chinese cultural society.

Useful organisation can also include *national bodies* with an interest in helping students from overseas, such as these, the addresses of which you'll find at the end of this book:—

UKCOSA; The British Council; The Commonwealth Institute.

Local contacts include: YMCA and YWCA; The International Friendship League (which is likely to have a local branch); Housing Advice Centre; Citizens' Advice Bureau.

15
Beyond college —
ready to leave?

Preparing to leave

Some time before the end of your final year issues about what to do next occur. Ideally, you'll have started to prepare yourself for life after college some time earlier, in the last term of your penultimate year or the first term of your final year. However, you may find you leave it until much later to decide what to do or to take active steps towards the future.

This final chapter alerts you to the options that exist for you and suggests ways in which you can set about getting help. It also overviews the job scene, your chances of getting a job and how college can fit in the context of your life.

Your main choices

These are the main choices you have at the end of your course. They are not mutually exclusive, for intance you can get a job abroad.

- A job
- Further study
- Going abroad
- Voluntary work
- Time out
- Unemployment
- Self-employment

A Job

If a job's what you want it's well worth knowing what employers are looking for and the state of the job scene.

What do employers look for?

Many employers are looking for evidence of ability and a degree of technical expertise. They want to recruit students who have studied particular subjects and gained at least a thorough grounding in that area, although most will want to train you in their way.

Employers are often concerned about the practical qualities of graduates. Although theoretical knowledge is not irrelevant, they want people who can tackle problems in the real world of work: what engineers often term 'hands on' people.

The quality of the degree can be important in many jobs but essential in others. Where this is important to employers, they may refer back to 'A' level grades as a guide to your likely degree/career performance, as is the case with some accountancy professions.

Employers increasingly seek numerate people, ie those who are not afraid of numbers and can use them in everyday working tasks, often with the aid of computers. Keyboard skills and computational understanding can also be useful.

Personal qualities in demand

Employers are seeking students who've made the most of their college life to develop themselves as people. Evidence of interesting use of vacations, part-time employment experience, an active and involved student life, sport or recreation and achievements will all be noted. They want the 'rounded' personality who can relate well to a wide group of people, communicate well in conversation and writing. They'll expect you to have some clear ideas about what you want from a career and to have equally clear reasons for wanting to work for them doing that particular job.

People who'll take responsibility and initiatives and who will be quick learners are also being sought. So too are flexible, adaptable people who are prepared to move around geographically, particularly in the early years of a career.

It all sounds rather daunting: 'Superstudent' step forward! It is, of course, what employers hope for as a composite ideal; for specific employers some of these qualities and skills are going to be more important than others.

Women and employment opportunities

By 1987 45% of those graduating from British colleges were women, a figure that continues to climb slowly. The signs are that women are doing slightly better in the graduate job market than men. In 1986, a slightly smaller proportion of women graduates were unemployed six months after graduation. They were doing at least as well as men in gaining postgraduate places.

Women are entering the fields of manufacturing industry and commercial areas such as accountancy, insurance and banking in increasing numbers. More women continue to enter teaching than men.

Despite the fact that women face discrimination in some employment fields, opportunities for career advancement are gradually improving.

Within the last decade the range and number of senior career posts held by women has substantially increased, even if there is still a long way to go before women take a full share of the top jobs in our society.

Minimising your chances of being unemployed
By carefully researching which course you will undertake before going to college, you can be clearer as to your job chances at the end of it, even given that employment prospects can change over a three, four or five year period. If you are studying a subject with a higher risk of unemployment at the end of it, some simple guidelines can minimise your chances of being unemployed.

● Be prepared to work at something entirely unrelated to your subject. This may well be difficult, particularly if you've enthusiasm and commitment to it. (This may be a contributory reason to some courses having higher unemployment rates — the reluctance to 'abandon' the subject.)

● Be prepared for a longer period of job searching than some others, with a period of short-term unemployment. Although many employers continue to recruit in the spring and summer, vacancies occur throughout the year.

● Be prepared to retrain by doing another vocationally-orientated course.

● Be aware that up to 40% of all vacancies are for graduates of *any* discipline. That is these employers are concerned about recruiting graduates irrespective of subject. They are more concerned about their personal qualities.

● Make the most of college life to develop yourself as a person, so that you may have a number of the qualities that an employer is looking for.

● Be prepared to take a job which under-employs you, ie which you don't need a degree or diploma to do. You can use it as a stepping stone up, or out of, the job. (Some employers are reluctant to offer such jobs to graduates, however. Be prepared to be told you're over qualified.)

Maximising your employment chances

Changes in the graduate employment scene occur regularly but there are some trends which help you both get a job and be well paid.

● Use your time at college to the full. Using clubs and societies, travel and vacations to the full, as well as working at your studies, can make a key difference to your job chances.

● The better your degree the better your job chances appear to be: 2.1 and 1st class honours graduates have the best employment records — but by no means do they automatically get jobs. Personal qualities of a 3rd class honours can outstrip a 2.1 graduate without the qualities.

● 24% of all vacancies for graduates in 1986 were those who'd studied Engineering and Technology. Those with Engineering, Physical Sciences and Business Studies degrees had among the lowest unemployment rates and a wide range of job opportunities.

● The university graduates were slightly better paid according to a 1986 survey by Manchester Polytechnic, which also found that those with a first class honours degree from a polytechnic were the best paid four years after graduation.

● There is a shortage of engineers and computer scientists and some evidence, in 1987, of shortages occuring in areas like physics, for those with degrees in these areas.

Good job news for graduates

● Employment prospects for all graduates have improved by the late 1980s after their slump in the early 80s, although they've not yet reached the heights of the mid 70s. 1987 was the best year of the 1980s.

● There are fewer graduates chasing more jobs, eg in 1987 a 3% higher level of job availability, with fewer graduates than in a peak year such as 1984/5.

● There are fewer applicants for many of the jobs advertised.

● It has become easier to leave job applications until later in the final year, as many employers recruit all the year round.

● Demand for graduates is growing among smaller companies, entering graduate recruitment for the first time. It is also growing in retailing, fast food and catering where some vacancies are unfilled.

● There is a continued rise in demand for graduates in the financial sector.

- The buoyant demand affects graduates of all disciplines, although non-numerate graduates in social services and humanities are among groups who may take longer to get a job, particularly with fewer jobs in the state sector.

- There is hardly any long-term unemployment among graduates. After 3 years nearly all graduates are in employment whatever degree they took. Most have fixed themselves up with a job or course within the year.

- Time out, for a year, is generally well regarded if constructively spent and particularly valuable if a job or course place is arranged beforehand.

The vital careers service

The college's career service with its careers advisers or counsellors and careers information staff are your fundamental tool in finding your way through these options. You can explore *time out* via files and reference books giving you ideas and contacts. You can find out about *further study, research grants* at home or abroad via prospectuses and reference works. Guides exist to *jobs abroad, voluntary work* and *self-employment* as well.

You'll find much more vital information and resources there. You can:—

- Book interviews with careers advisers.

- Find details of tens of thousands of job vacancies with thousands of employers.

- Attend careers education programmes which will help you look at yourself, your decisions and your application and interview skills.

- Be interviewed by employers visiting the college on 'milk rounds', as they are called.

- Get free graduate guides — large volumes called GO, GET, and DOG, which give you a clear picture of the demand for graduates from employers.

- Collect free self-help materials on *how* to set about applying, with guidance on letters, curriculum vitae (cv), interview technique, etc.

- Pick up AGCAS/CSU careers information booklets giving you guidance of main graduate careers.

- Find prospectuses for hundreds of firms and application forms for them.

College in the context of your life

It is often not until you look back on an experience that you begin to see it in perspective. Initially, you may find that you'll experience a sense of loss when you first leave college. It will take time to unwind from being a student. The support from friends and the college may now be absent and fending for yourself as you enter or seek employment can feel tough.

Although friends tend to disperse all over the country at the end of their college lives, good friends will stay in contact for many years. College friendships are often lasting ones as the experiences you have been through together have been so important to you. Some colleges have societies for ex-students and some form of mailing system, but many don't. Many people you've known will fade from the memory as you'll never see them again.

You may meet course members again when the awards ceremony occurs, usually in the November/December in the year you complete the course. This will be one opportunity to revisit the old place, dress up and compare notes. A substantial minority of students stay on in the local town or city and either take a break after the course or use the town as a base for a job search whilst on the dole. This keeps some continuity of contact with people and places for a short time at least.

College days are likely to be among the most significant in your life. The whole experience is likely to affect the way in which you live your life — your job, your relationships and where you are able to live. You will have the opportunity to do so many different things. The moans about the college, the course work, the SU, and so on, may seem surprising in retrospect when you reminisce about the good times you've had. Hopefully, you will have had many more good times than bad.

Superstudent

Useful Reading

Acres, David, *How to pass Exams Without Anxiety,* Northcote House Publishers, 1987.

Acres, David, *How to Get to College.*

AGCAS, *What do Graduates Do?*

Aliston, A and Miller, R, *Equal Opportunities — A Careers Guide.*

Ashman, S and George, A, *Study and Learn.*

British Council, *How to Live in Britain.*

Cadwallader, S and Ohr, J, *Whole Earth Cookbook.*

Central Bureau for Educational Visits and Exchanges, *Working Holidays.*

Cocker, David, *Successful Exam Technique,* Northcote House Publishers, 1987.

CRAC, *A Year Off.*

CRAC, *Student Life.*

CSU, *University Graduates.*

DES, *Grants to Students.*

Family Welfare Association, *Charities Digest.*

Fletcher, Joan, *How to Get That Job,* Northcote House Publishers, 1987.

Gabbitas-Thring Guide to Independent Further Education, Northcote House Publishers, 1987.

HMSO/DHSS, *Going to College or University? A pocket guide to social security.*

HMSO, *Graduates and Jobs.*

Innes, J, *The Pauper's Cookbook.*

Jones, Alan, *Successful Interview Technique,* Northcote House Publishers, 1988.

King, Elizabeth, *How to Use a Library,* Northcote House Publishers, 1987.

Knight, J (ed), *Graduate Studies.*

Lock, D and Lotinga, H (ed), *The Campus Cookbook.*

NUS, *Educational Charities. A Guide to Educational Trust Funds.*

NUS, *Undergraduate Income and Expenditure Survey.*

Rathfelder, Martin, *How to Claim State Benefits,* Northcote House Publishers, 1987.

Segal, A (ed), *The Careers Encyclopedia.*

Glossary

Advisory interview. An interview with a college or employer to give you guidance as to what steps you can take: it is not a selection interview.

AGCAS. Association of Graduate Careers Advisory Services. Provides guidance and information services for universities and polytechnics.

AGR. Association of Graduate Recruiters (formerly SCOEG). A body of employers of graduates who work closely with AGCAS.

CAB. Citizens' Advice Bureau.

Campus. The college site.

College. The term used through the book to cover universities, polytechnics, colleges of higher education and colleges of art.

CNAA. Council for National Academic Awards.

Course work. Work to be completed during the student year which often counts towards the overall assessment.

CRAC. Careers Research and Advisory Council. Publish useful career materials.

CSU. Central Services Unit. Information distribution service for higher education careers services.

DES. Department of Education and Science.

DHSS. Department of Health and Social Security.

Digs. Accommodation provided in another person's home, with some meals provided.

DipHE. Diploma in Higher Education.

Discontinue. To drop out of college voluntarily.

Discretionary grant award. A grant that a local authority does not have to pay unless it feels the circumstances merit it.

Enrolment. The process of signing up officially as a college student.

Fees. Payments for course tuition and examinations.

Fieldwork. Practical work as part of a course, applying theory to a real situation.

Foundation courses. Introductory courses, often of one year's duration, to more specialist fields, eg Art.

Freshers. New first year students in a college.

Further education. Refers generally to all post-compulsory education after 16 but more specifically to 16-19 education.

Hall of residence. A residential block for students providing, minimally, study bedrooms and shared catering, toilet and washing facilities.

Higher education. Post 'A' level (or equivalent) education, usually for those aged above 18.

HND. Higher National Diploma. A 2 year full-tme course (longer if a sandwich course) in higher education with a practical applicability.

Induction. The process of helping students settle into college. May involve courses, talks, social events, etc.

LEA. Local education authority. The body responsible for paying grants and fees for students to attend college.

Mandatory grant award. A grant which the LEA has no choice but to offer a student.

Masters degree. Usually a postgraduate qualification although there are some exceptions, eg Scotland (a first degree) and Oxbridge (can be purchased to 'top up' your first degree).

Mature student. For grant purposes, 'mature' means over 25. Otherwise any students who have taken a break between earlier full time education and full-time study.

NUS. National Union of Students. The representative body for students to which the majority of Students Unions are affiliated.

Oxbridge. The combined name for Oxford and Cambridge Universities.

Parental contribution. The amount parents would have to contribute to their child's grant to bring it up to the maximum LEA provision.

PCAS. Polytechnic Central Admissions System.

PhD. Doctor of Philosophy. A postgraduate qualification also known as a doctorate.

Placement. A period of practical work which is an integral part of a course.

Postgraduate. A student studying for any qualification after a first degree or diploma.

Prospectus. A free booklet issued by a college describing the college, courses and entrance procedures.

Rag. The college students' yearly opportunity for being very silly for one or two weeks in stunts and social events to raise money for charity.

Redbrick. The name used to describe provincial universities.

Refectory. A self-service canteen.

Resits. A second chance to sit, normally one or two, failed exams a few weeks after the original exams.

Sandwich course. A course with a period away from college to gain practical experience and further training.

Seminar. A small group discussion in which students take an active role.

Sponsorship. A payment made in whole or part by an actual or potential employer towards the cost of a student studying.

SU. Students Union. The representative body of a college.

Study skills. The skills of learning how to study.

Supplementary benefit. Money that may be claimed from the DHSS.

Undergraduate. A student on a first degree course.

Viva. An oral examination.

Warden. A member of college staff responsible for students in halls.

YMCA/YWCA. Young Men's/Women's Christian Association. Often used as residences by students.

Further Useful Addresses

Central Registrar and Clearing
  House Ltd
3 Crawford Place
London WH1 2BM

Committee of Directors of
  Polytechnics
309 Regent Street
London W1R 7PE

Commonwealth Institute
230 Kensington High Street
London W8 6NQ
Tel: 01-603 4535

Council for National
  Academic Awards
344-354 Gray's Inn Road
London WC1X 8BP
Tel: 01-278 4411

Education Grants Advisory Service
501 Kinglands Road
London E8

Manpower Services Commission
Administrative Head Office
Press and Information Office
Selkirk House
High Holborn
London WC1
Tel: 01-836 1213

National Bureau for Handicapped
  Students
40 Brunswick Square
London WC1N 1AZ
Tel: 01-278 3450

National Council for Civil Liberties
186 Kings Cross Road
London WC1
Tel: 01-278 4575

National Union of Students
3 Endsleigh Street
London WC1
Tel: 01-387 1277
or
3 Marton Road
London N16
Tel: 01-429 8008

Overseas Student Services
  Department
The British Council
11 Portland Place
London W1N 4EJ

Release
1 Elgin Avenue
London W9 3PR
Tel: 01-603 8654

Scottish Education Department
Dover House
Whitehall
London SW1A 2AY
Tel: 01-233 2000

Universities' Central Council on
  Admissions
PO Box 28
Cheltenham
Gloucestershire GL50 1HY

Vacation Work Publications
9 Park End Street
Oxford OX1 1JH

Voluntary Service Overseas
9 Belgrave Square
London SW1X 8PW

Index